Sworn In

The career of Officer 1481

By

Jeremy H Cohen

2019

ISBN: 9781092862264

Jeremy H Cohen

Sworn In

Dedication

I would like to take a moment to dedicate this book as an expression of my utmost thanks and ongoing support to all of the Law Enforcement Officers the world over, it is a truly unique and challenging job. One that requires, professionalism, restraint, bravery, a warped sense of humour & good friends to help you through the day to day tasks. If I ever see one of you in trouble, rest assured I'm coming to help!

I would like to express my support for the East Anglian Air Ambulance, the incredible charity that helps save lives day after day, and also to the Addenbrookes Hospitals' NCCU (Neurosciences Critical Care Unit), the people who provide world-class care for those with critical head injuries.

To my friends and colleagues at Suffolk Constabulary. Those that were there when I called for help, those that sat and had a tea with me (and the occasional biscuit!), those that laughed with me (and at me!), those that held me and said *"See you soon"* on my last day, those that are my friends. I love you all.

And finally to my family, who had to put up with my ever-changing moods, my long hours, and my never relenting cynicism. Without you there for me, I would not be the person I am today; a loving husband, a caring father, a grateful son and an annoying brother.

Sworn In

Be Forewarned!

I have never been that politically correct and I have a strange, dark sense of humour. I do swear, I do curse, I am very cynical, I am sarcastic, I hate laziness and incompetence infuriates me. And to top it all off, I say what I think, often making those around me cringe in horror!

You will be pleased to hear though, that I hate and despise criminals. Those taking things belonging to others, those making people live in fear of burglary and those that risk the lives of others on the road, I hate the lot of them!

What follows are accounts of real-life incidents. I have purposefully kept some details out as a way of protecting those involved, it was hard enough for them as it was!

Finally, I tell it like it was. I have been descriptive, there are accounts telling of major injuries, some proving fatal, others not. After all, I am doing this in the hope you can see what emergency service personnel deal with day in, day out, and to raise awareness of the possible side effects when exposed to this repeated major trauma.

But, before we move on I must add....*That any views, expressed or implied are that of my own, they in no way imply the thoughts, opinions or actions of any other person or public service.......*still with me?? Good, then let's double crew together!

Sworn In

On a dark, damp and cold evening, the haze of blue lights are flickering on the road in front, the flashing of blue is reflecting against the hedgerows, the occupants of the unlit houses you pass are sleeping peacefully unaware anything has gone on, the police radio is constantly going off in your ear, you are desperately listening for any updates, imaging the worst, but hoping for the best. What will I be presented with? You're hoping other officers are on their way too…Are the occupants dead? How will I tell the family? What if I know them? What condition is the person's body going to be in…? You're en route to a serious collision, and the initial call was; *"It looks bad, there's lots of blood and the drivers not moving…"*

As you arrive, your headlights slowly illuminate the scene, gradually unwrapping the incident like a story for you to read. Debris and oil are strewn all over the road, people are pacing about in a mad panic, rushing over as soon you arrive, they want your help - you can solve this, you can make this all better they are hoping. You can see a car that is heavily impacted into a tree on the verge, the front end has been crumpled up to the cockpit like it's been in a crusher, leaving the tree now standing where the gear stick should be, almost cutting the car in two.

Your heart is racing, a million thoughts are going through your mind at once, how? What should I do first? Are these people involved too? How many people are in the car? I have got to get the road closed, take witness statements, identify the occupant if they are in fact dead….You're not even out of the car yet!

You open the door and fling on your coat, with the first aid box in one hand, the camera hanging around your neck and paperwork under your arm, you walk towards the scene.

The crashed cars' horn is on a constant wail and everyone is speed talking at you all at the same time, *"GIVE ME A SECOND!!!!!"* you want to shout.

Blanking everyone you approach the car, it is a complete wreck, anyone in there must be in a mess. Looking closer you can just make out a lifeless body crumpled up in amongst the twisted grey and oily metal. Still approaching you suddenly think, is any petrol leaking? And I must get my rubber gloves on!

Now standing at the side of the car, you bend down to the narrow gap that used to be the front window. You can see blood all over the driver's ashen coloured face which has a vacant and lifeless expression. The smell of blood and oil are filling your nostrils as you reach out and touch their shoulder, and with apprehension filling your stomach you call out;

"Hello???? Can you hear me???"
……………………………………..……………….Nothing!!

This would fast become my daily life, but first, a bit about me.

I was employed by Suffolk Constabulary, a rural police force covering a county that has a population nearing 1 million residents spread throughout the history-rich 1,466sq miles of area[1]. It is both an extremely busy and yet also a beautifully peaceful place to work, visit and live.

With recorded crime rates roughly between 55,000-75,000 crimes per year, plus the non-recorded crime incidents; crashes, suicides, sudden deaths, missing people reports (mispers) and mental health jobs etc.… all requiring police attendance and roughly 140,000 emergency 999 calls and around 270,000 non-emergency calls per year, you can see that for a small place, it was quite busy!

I worked for the Constabulary for over 13 years, 4 of which was as a local patrol officer in the busy and overcrowded town of Ipswich, then 1 year based at Hadleigh in a small rural station before achieving my dream of working on the Roads Policing Unit, where I worked for just over 8 years before needing to change the direction in my life. If I'm honest, there's only so much a person can take.

Throughout my career, I was repeatedly exposed to major trauma, heartbreak and upset, but at the same time a lot of joy and happiness too. Some of the jobs I was involved in made local and national news, some even made international news. Then there were the ones that wouldn't even interest a cat, I will not bore you with those!

So why am I doing this? I have a few reasons, I'd like to document my career so that when I'm old and senile my daughters might read this book and discover an aspect of my life they are at present too young to understand and appreciate. I'm also hoping to give more people an insight into the life of a modern-day British Police officer, although I dare say, this will be typical the world over. Maybe you are considering a career in the Police Force, or have a relative in the Force, or are just interested in another part of the world around you, one that is often confined to the stories of the press.

Police officers are trained to expect and deal with major incidents suddenly and without any prior warning. There is no email, no phone call, no meeting and no memo. It is something that happens out of the blue. It could be a death on the road, a violent offender, a murder, a rape, a child abuse incident, a suicide, basically anything on the higher end of the scale can be thrust your way at any given moment.

Dealing with these kinds of incidents on a regular basis makes it normal for an experienced officer to walk into and even seek out the high trauma incidents as though it is perfectly normal. It is honestly as though anything less traumatic didn't get you as focused as they used to, and did actually bore you! For example, once I was established within the Roads Policing Unit and had to attend an "everyday" collision, I used to find myself saying to my colleagues afterwards; *"That was a crap crash."*

It is an amazing concept that someone can deal with something that to the victim, is hopefully a once in a lifetime horrific incident and yet was almost a non-event for a seasoned officer. Police officers are also the only people I know who get that use to dealing with these kind of tragedies, that they can stand over a dead decaying corpse and happily discuss what they are going to have for refs and talk about their plans for after their shift ends, just like many other occupations get used to staring at a computer screen in the safety an office block, and think about their lunch or plans for the evening. Police officers are unique, and through their daily work become very conditioned people.

But before we get in too deep, how did I get here? And what was my background?

Now in my mid to late '30s, I grew up in a quiet rural village. My dad was a Reverend in the local church and my mother was a teacher, I had a younger sister, an older brother and a dog. A normal everyday family, but as with most families, pull back the wrapping and things can be significantly more interesting.

I was adopted into my family as a baby and grew up playing outside, climbing trees and digging in the dirt, all of the good things that kids should do! My sister was born to my mum and dad and my brother was adopted from yet another family.

I was quite a shy and introvert person and suffered badly with social anxiety, which I still do. I would later come to realise that my Police uniform was acting as my cape of confidence, with it on I could approach anyone or any incident with the confidence in my own abilities and knowledge of the laws I was enforcing, take it off and I return to my "Clark Kent" a quiet, shy and often insecure person.

I preferred having my own space and I loved the freedom of being outdoors. Given my later chosen career, my traits didn't really go with my first impressions of what a Police officer was like. I hated change and unpredictability with a passion.

My dad died following a long illness when I was in my teens, something I did not deal with well, I never talked about it or expressed my emotions to anyone.

My older brother moved out of the family home and chose a path that would lead me to want to have nothing much to do with him. My sister was incredibly close to my mum and remains that way today, she is now a teacher like my mum was.

I finished school with average grades, GCSE grade C's and then went to an Agricultural College at Otley in Suffolk to study Horticulture and Sports Turf technology. I spent 2 years there before finally passing the course with a Merit.

After college, I managed to secure a job as a Greenkeeper at Hintlesham Hall Championship Golf course and worked there for about 4 years, it was a great job, providing fresh air, exercise and the freedom to move around and not be stuck in a dreaded office.

One love of my life was driving, and on the Golf course I got to drive all kinds of different things, tractors, all-terrain vehicles and the huge ride on gang mowers, anything, anywhere, anytime, don't know why, but I got an immense sense of enjoyment out of it. The only problem with the job being, it was not paying enough money to move out of the family home and get a decent mortgage on a house outside of town and in the countryside.

I looked into a number of options and was left with the idea of joining the Police Force. I obtained an application form for the local Constabulary, filled it out and sent it in.

Whilst waiting on a reply I entered into a civilian driving course with the Institute of Advanced Motorists, It would be a small insight into the Police driving system, called Roadcraft. I passed this easily and was presented my certificate by His Highness the Duke of Gloucester, the Queen's cousin.

After a number of weeks, and very much to my surprise, I got accepted for the next stage in the Police application process, an assessment centre with interviews and roleplays. I was dreading this, being judged and doing things in front of people, I knew my comfort zone was going to get stretched!! Something I would have to get used to.

Assessment day came and I was dressed smartly wearing a suit, which I hated! I have this personal belief that when you put a suit on a man, even a good friendly man, he turns into a complete self-important arse! Like he's wearing a cape of arrogance.

I had spent many hours trawling the internet finding out information on the Constabulary, but I was still feeling totally underprepared for what was coming and thought that I must stick out dreadfully in this kind of environment. I was sure to arrive with plenty of time to spare just in case of any unforeseen issues, and to allow numerous trips to the bathroom for a nervous wee!

Once at the Police Headquarters I signed in at the reception and was taken to sit in a long corridor where Police memorabilia, historic uniforms, medals, trophies and pictures adorned the walls and the many display cabinets, the sense you had entered an important and history-rich organisation was there for all to see.

I was one of about 20 people sat in a line of chairs waiting to be called for my first test, my stomach was doing summersaults and I was in a major internal panic. As time passed people were being called away and would then return a while later, it would eventually be my turn. My name was called and I was taken to another section of the building, where I was told I was not to discuss the tests with any of the other candidates. I would then participate in a couple of role-play scenarios, designed to show how you speak to people in different situations.

I was given a printed card with a brief summary of a scenario that described what had happened on it, which I had to memorise. Then I was released into another room to deal with the described incident, no policing knowledge was needed, it was more a test of personality and how you can adapt.

I then completed a maths test, a written test (writing a lengthy letter) and had a really odd first interview. The interviewer was scripted, reading from a card asking questions only, there was no replies and no chit chat, just question answer, question answer, it felt really weird and uncomfortable.

I went away at the end of the day with a genuine feeling of having been on a train and just going along with what was happening, I didn't have the *"I thought I did well / bad"* thoughts going through my mind, it was just quite a bizarre day for me.

After a few weeks, I heard that I had been successful and would now be invited for a medical examination and fitness test – the fitness test back then was an actual test!! – With me still working on the golf course coupled with the fact I had been working on my fitness and strength, I didn't have any issues with this and both were completed with no worries, now I would be moving on to the next stage.

A few weeks later, I received a letter inviting me for a final interview, this was the important one, the time to show senior ranked officers who I am and why they should select me over the other people. I again arrived in plenty of time and was invited into a briefing room. There were 5 people sat in a row behind a desk, with a lone chair in the centre of the room for me to sit at. I did not like how this felt, again, no policing knowledge was needed.

I was asked why I wanted to join the police and in particular that force, what I expected the repercussions on my personal life to be, and how I would handle certain incidents and situations. This was much more of a two-way conversation than the weird interview a few weeks earlier. This time though I left there feeling I had messed that up completely!

One question was, *"You are walking in the street and someone covered in blood approaches you saying they've been attacked, you then see a person brandishing a bloody knife. What do you do?"* Well, I answered the question as best I could, then when I was driving out of the car park on my way home, I had a sudden and very deflating thought – *"I forgot to get the injured person an ambulance!!!!! Police protect life and limb, I'd completely messed that up!"*

A few weeks later and again to my amazement, I got another letter saying I had been successful through the application phase, pending background checks and I was to attend for a uniform fitting. I couldn't believe it! I felt on top of the moon.

The date came and I got fitted for my Police uniform at the Police Headquarters uniform store. Being amongst the rows and rows of new uniform I felt in total awe at the history I was now becoming part of. Following this, I was advised to wait for a training start date and not to hand my resignation in at the golf course until a start date had been given.

The uniform when I started consisted of; a white cotton long/short sleeve shirt, a black clip-on tie, hideous thick black cotton/polyester trousers, a navy blue woollen jumper, black ankle boots, an upper body armour (stab vest), a custodian helmet, a flat cap, a utility belt to hold the appointments – handcuffs, extendable baton and CS incapacitant spray. We were also given a smart black tunic for court and other official occasions, and also a number of different thickness high-vis yellow jackets.

A couple of weeks had passed without any word from the Constabulary, and then out of the blue, my world collapsed!! I received another letter, apparently, I had now been unsuccessful in my application due to background checks into a member of my family! I was livid, this person's life and own choices had now stopped me in my tracks, and I hated the person!

I lodged an appeal to the Constabulary, and my Uncle also lodged one to the local Member of Parliament Tim Yeo, telling them about me and my character and that I have nothing to do with and in fact despised this idiot. After a good few weeks, I'd heard nothing and gave up. I carried on at the golf course wondering where to take my life now.

A couple of months later I was at work, sat having my refs break in the tea room when I heard the phone ring and a minute later my boss called me into his office, *"The Chief Constable is on the phone for you,"* in a state of disbelief and also shell shock I took the phone, it was him! The top officer of the force! He talked to me about my hopes for the Police Force and how I had done at the assessments, he then offered me the Office of Police Constable, if I would still like it, and, on the proviso I sign a letter stating I will never reside or co-habit with that member of my family whilst employed by the Constabulary, even for one night. Easy!!!!! Absolutely!!!!!!!

The emotional rollercoaster continued, I received another letter, this time with a start date on it. I handed in my notice to the Golf Club, which had been a brilliant place to work and a place where I got to know some really great people. I still talk about it today and visit when I can.

In March 2005 I joined Suffolk Constabulary.

Tunic and Custodian helmet. March/April 2005. © Jeremy H Cohen

The first aspect of the training was a few weeks based at the Police headquarters in Martlesham. This was completely residential with the whole intake residing in the same block. It was a great way to get to know your future colleagues and by staying on the premises 24/7 provided me with the time to get accustomed to the world of Policing that I was now entering.

There were ground rules mind you! No Alcohol allowed and no cohabiting in a bedroom!! A few items of contraband did manage to find their way in though, obviously!

Class time was to get some basics under our belt, minor offences, getting used to the protective equipment – extendable baton or ASP, CS-Spray and handcuffs, learning the functions of the digital radios and covering some general policing duties.

Towards the end of the residential period, we had our swearing-in ceremony, the moment we would officially be becoming an officer and this would also be the first time out in public wearing a Police Uniform.

Wearing a crisply ironed white shirt, trousers, a tie, my Police custodian hat, tunic and polished boots we all entered the Ipswich Magistrates court in procession, walking past a group of lads who were smoking by the doorway and all wearing grey tracksuits and swearing as we passed. Later in my career, these people would become known to me as *"Scrotes!"* A contemptible person, a gobshite and a criminal. A waste of space and a burden to society. I could feel them staring at us all as we walked past them, for the first time in my life I felt like an enemy, hated and despised purely for the uniform I now wore, and that I would soon become a hazard to their occupation of being a criminal. It was truly a strange and nerve-wracking feeling as I had not knowingly been around criminals before, this feeling was one I'll remember forever.

One by one we took our place before the head magistrate,

"I, Jeremy Cohen of Suffolk Constabulary do solemnly and sincerely declare and affirm that I will well and truly serve the Queen in the office of constable, with fairness, integrity, diligence and impartiality, upholding fundamental human rights and

according equal respect to all people; and that I will, to the best of my power, cause the peace to be kept and preserved and prevent all offences against people and property; and that while I continue to hold the said office I will to the best of my skill and knowledge discharge all the duties thereof faithfully according to law."[2]

That's it, I was now Police Constable 1481 and had full Police powers in the whole of England, Wales and the adjacent waters!!! Albeit on a leash, I still had the training to do!

We would then soon be off to one of the national Police training centres, but first, the instructors thought it a good idea for us to experience the CS spray on ourselves. We all stood in a line at the back of HQ and an instructor walked past us discharging CS canisters into our faces, what a lovely feeling that was! Nose running everywhere, eyes stinging and watering, my throat sore and itchy, it was bloody horrible.

Ashford Police Training Centre, Kent.
What an incredible place, the main building Grosvenor Hall was built in 1875 and had many previous uses until taken over for use by the Police for training in 1973. It comprised of small mock town that to the people who have been there was known as Sandford. For training purposes, it had a specially built bar, houses, roads, bus stops, classes, open areas and a large parade square. The Residential blocks ran along the edge of the site with blocks for the men and blocks for the women, I spent my 12 weeks there in a shared Dorm with 2 others.

The training centre had a fully kitted out gym, bar, disco hall, snooker room, canteen, sports hall and fields, swimming pool, a few private TV rooms and more, for us all to use and enjoy in our downtime.

One aspect that would take some getting used to mind you, was the ablutions in the residential block, a back to back row of sinks that ran along the middle of the room, a line of showers on one wall and a line of toilets on the other wall. Now, if you're anything like me, going to the toilet is a private affair, I don't want to talk to anyone and I don't want to be heard...The thought of re-enacting the famous scene from the movie Austin Powers, *("Who does number 2 work for?!!")* with strangers in cubicles next to me was not a nice thought. I guess this was more of the breaking down of those comfort zones!!

The training centre was staffed by Serving and ex-Police officers from around the South-East of England. Constabularies from that same area would send their new recruits to learn the laws and put them into practice in the safety of the Police grounds.

Meeting people from other Forces added a greater sense of the *"Police Family"* that kept being spoken of, for me this was the best way to ready new officers for the street. Sadly, this doesn't happen anymore and it's all in-house in an attempt to save money, and the training centre was demolished to make way for a new residential housing estate. These newer officers, in my opinion, lack the experience that comes from going into the world of a large training centre, with a lot of new people and places they don't know, sharing Dorms, learning to live with others who are initially strangers, forming bonds with people and creating life stories. It is to this day a saying of mine, *"If you don't have stories to tell, you haven't lived,"* or as it was so well put in the TV series Downton Abbey; *"The business of life is the acquisition of memories."*

I would travel down each Sunday afternoon and return home each Friday afternoon, luckily in the company of a new friend I had now made, who made great company on the long journeys back and forth, providing an interesting range of conversations.

My class was made up of a few people from my local force and some from the other forces present, there were 14 recruits and 2 dedicated trainers making up our particular class, Class J7/2005.

The typical day would start at 6-7am in the large canteen with a self-serve breakfast, a choice of cereals, toast, hot food and fruit. From there we would shower, shave and get dressed, then go to some morning classes covering varying topics of law, and then, to lunch, again in the canteen for a light meal of sandwiches, fruits, salads and yoghurts. After lunch would tend to be role-play scenarios making good use of the constructed town to play out the laws we'd been learning in the morning sessions, and how as a Police officer you'd deal with the different scenarios presented to you.

Anything to do with rioting was my least favourite, helmet and safety gear on, having things thrown at you and trying to instil peace and order into a rabid group of people hell-bent on bowling you over and burning you alive with Molotov cocktails, that was not my kind of thing at all! Being in large crowds and having to push towards those attacking you with objects and weapons did not seem fun! Luckily being part of the riot police (PSU) was an optional extra for those that wanted it, I wouldn't.

The more sedentary scenarios tended to focus on minor offences such as thefts. You would wait in a room and then receive a call via your radio about a theft from a shop or similar, and then you would take the long quiet walk to the scenario location, the whole time the theft definition going through your head.

The Theft Act 1968 –*"a person is guilty of theft if they dishonestly appropriate property belonging to another with the intention to permanently deprive the other of it."*

This was one of many definitions we had to know verbatim and everyone it seemed had their own way of learning them, mine was by rote, using a book called "The Beat Officers Companion" by Janes Police Handbooks. It became a friend to me and it went everywhere, I'd even find myself asking where my book named *"Jane"* was sometimes.

We would have a fair bit of PST (Personal Safety Training), this would involve the use of the baton, handcuff's, incapacitant spray and your own body going through restraint techniques, self-defence and non-compliant arrest scenarios, this was a new world to me, learning to hurt people (when needed) and to protect yourself, it began what I still consider a life-changing knowledge and one that is good to know in your personal life, not just within the Police.

With the British Police still being primarily unarmed, for reasons dating back to the time when the Metropolitan Police Force was founded in 1892, on the principle of policing by the consent of the public and not by dictatorship or force of the state, coupled with the ever real and climbing knife attack rates, self-defence training had to be taken seriously. And in the current day, according to GunPolicy.org, "only 4 people own a gun out of every 100" (that are legally registered and known about!!), so it is believed to be unnecessary to arm all British officers, A subject which draws large arguments both for and against amongst the public and also the Police.

The downside to this training was people would often get carried away, causing many injuries and providing a real appreciation for the pain these techniques and equipment could inflict on someone.

When role-playing as a baddy with a set rigid cuffs on your wrist, and the person being the officer was throwing you down to the floor with too much realism, the feeling of *"Is my wrist broken because it bloody HURTS!"* would be commonplace.

The training which covered close combat training, defence against knife attacks and dog attacks etc. would then be repeated every 6 months for the rest of my career.

The day would end at about 4.30pm-5pm and I would often go and squeeze in a quick swim before heading to the canteen for dinner. A row of large vats full of hearty meals, casserole, stew, sausage and Veg to name a few, there were lighter options, but I never had those. There was then the pudding vats, sponge and custard, bread and butter pudding, pie, everything it seemed. And I always had seconds!! I loved meal time at Ashford, a chance to discuss your day and stuff yourself stupid.

After dinner, the social side kicked in, if you wanted it to. Some people would go to the bar, the gym or TV rooms. I often went to the snooker hall with a couple of people and then went to the bar to have a drink, play games, chat, and generally enjoy my life and the new friendships I was now forming. Some nights my little "click" would forego dinner and head out of the grounds and go to Ashford Town itself, to enjoy the cinema, local pubs and the infamous "liquid nightclub." It was also the scene of my very first Doner Kebab! Something that should be disgusting and was dreadful for you, but was in-fact bloody lovely. After the stresses and mental strains of the day, a relaxing evening was badly needed. I had started to learn a new feeling in life, being mentally exhausted! It was often into bed by 10-11pm to feel fresh enough for the next day of new laws and practices.

There were continual assessments both practical and written, when these came up everyone was getting up earlier in the morning to study and also forgoing the recreation in the evening to make sure there was no need for a re-sit. Luckily I have always been fine when put under pressure for tests and passed these with relative ease, although I did make my own luck by putting in the time to study when needed.

During some of our lunch breaks, we would be out on the Parade Square going through the routine of marching and presenting, all to be ready for our final day when we have to parade before the chief constables and other dignitaries. Fortunately, one of our classmates that had served in the military took great pride in leading us through this showcase and readied us for the final day.

On our last night, there was a leaving disco and buffet, it was a very enjoyable night with people going over stories of the past weeks and wishing new found friends well for when they get out on patrol.

We ended our time at Ashford with a class photo and then the parade. It was a hot, clear and sunny day, we were all dressed smartly, shoes polished and had not a hair out of place, we stood to attention and motionless on the square for just over 3 long and very hot hours. A couple of people, unfortunately, fainted due to a mixture of too much alcohol at the disco, the heat and slowing blood circulation to the head. One way of combatting this was to wiggle your toes and do the typical 'Policeman's bob' – to do this you slightly raise your flat feet onto the front of the foot by lifting your heel and then going back down again, very small, but necessary movements, all in the hope of keeping the blood circulating back up to the head properly and therefore avoiding the fainting episodes.

ASHFORD INITIAL COURSE J/2005
Class J7 with me bottom left. © R. Carley Police Training Photography.

I will forever look back at my time at Ashford with a smile and the knowledge that I achieved what was required to move on in the Police training regime.

It would then be back to the Constabulary to learn local procedures, reinforce the laws learnt and do ever more role-play scenarios.

On July 7th 2005, our training, unfortunately, came to an unexpected and horrible halt. A coordinated terrorist attack had occurred in London, where the bombings of the underground train network and an over-ground bus by extremists was carried out, this left 52 members of the public dead and 784 people suffering from non-fatal injuries[3]. The mental injuries suffered to families, witnesses and emergency services personnel will probably never be fully quantified. I can distinctly remember the news channels filled with the horrific footage from the scene, seeing people in distress brought on by people for no good reason at all was sickening.

As a result of this incident, phone lines were set up around the UK, these were to be known as casualty bureaus. A service members of the public could call to register a friend or family member as missing, not heard from, and in the area concerned. My Constabulary set one of these up and utilised me and my course to be the call takers, we had strict instructions on what was to be done and how.

Sat in a room with 14 phones, one per desk we would answer the call stating the caller had reached the Casualty Bureau for the London bombings of July 7th 2005. Then, using a thick form (more like a book), called a disaster victim identification form (DVI), we would try to obtain as much detail about the caller as possible and then move on to the person they were notifying us of, we needed their name, description, tattoos, clothes, personal belongings, where there went, where they were going, when last heard from, objects which could be obtained to secure DNA samples and much more. Often the caller was in tears and regularly hysterical, it was hard to gain this information without them being upset, because at the end of the day we wanted the information to help identify on a preliminary basis, bodies or bits of bodies, and the caller would have known that.

It was a very emotionally draining process. The phones never stopped ringing for the few days we did this and I would challenge anyone to hear the desperation in all those peoples voices knowing their friend or relative may be dead whilst you go through intimate information with them, without feeling desperately moved by it all.

I kept watching the news every evening to see the advancements made at the scene, and the photos appearing of those confirmed as dead. There were 2 people for which I took a call about appear on the screen as confirmed deceased, and that left a strange feeling of sadness and yet joy that I had done my job well, and also, a strange thought that I had only spoken to someone about them not that long ago.

The recruit training then continued in earnest, the next memorable part for me was a day out on the street with officers from the station where I was going to be based at. For me, it was the county town called Ipswich which has a population of around 180,000 residents. I started the day with a guided tour of the Police station and found it incredible that at the time, what would seem like a complete maze of rooms and corridors would soon become a regular place of mine.

I met the Scene of Crime Officers, then called SOCO, the CID department, custody staff and also looked around the towns cellblock which had 21 cells all ready to house between 6000-8000 detainees annually, (at the time the county of Suffolk as a whole received around 15,000-18,000 detainees on average per year, a number that would drop with the introduction of the new custody suites in the future to around 10,000-14,000 detainees). We also met with the Chief Officer of the station and the shift supervisors (Sergeants) currently on duty.

It was then time for lunch. Afterwards, I was introduced to two officers whom I'd be spending the afternoon with, I was lucky enough to be teamed with the town's area car.

The Area car, as it was then, but not anymore! Was generally 2 of the more experienced and productive officers on a shift who would not have workloads of jobs to investigate and would have completed the Police advanced driving course. They would be the primary response to any grade "A" incidents for their area, these would be incidents requiring an immediate emergency response. They would be sent anywhere around the town and the immediate outskirts, whereas the other town officers had smaller patches to patrol. If an incident occurred in your patch you would go to the incidents also, but the area car got to hand the job to the others once it was calm and then be ready to respond to the next emergency. Thus ensuring someone was always free to attend.

One incident we went to was a report of a mini moto (tiny motorcycle) being ridden around one of the housing estates, and the rider was not wearing a helmet. Not too bad on the face of it, but mini moto's were fast becoming a tool for criminals to get from job to job quicker than by bicycle, but still having the capability of getting through little gaps which a car wouldn't. So, when one when was seen in particular estates it was a fair bet the rider was up to no good, committing a crime and/or causing a public nuisance. On top of all this, there was also an obvious danger to the rider, other road users and the laws already being broken by it being used on the road.

These incidents would become rife for a short time before the next fad took over.

We went flying across the town in search of it, but never found it, for me though, it was the first time I'd been in an emergency vehicle on a blue light run so I loved it nonetheless. I would not be doing any driving myself mind you until my first police driving course, which I was really looking forward to!

Our initial training period ended without any glamour or ceremony and we merely moved on to the next part, now I was out on the street! With a tutor officer.

I turned up at my station and was allocated my lockers for kit, clothing and paperwork. I met my supervisor and also met my tutor, an experienced constable I would now spend 10 weeks with, hopefully following that I would then get authorised to patrol alone.

The shift pattern we primarily worked was known as a 2-2-2. It was 2-day shifts – 7 am to 5 pm, 2-late shifts – 4 pm to midnight, or until 3 am on Thursday, Friday and Saturday, and 2-night shifts – 11 pm to 7 am. We would then have 4 days off before the cycle continued.

My shift consisted of 2 Sergeants and 10 constables for the town of Ipswich and the surrounding housing estates.

I got to know my tutor well, and loved my time with him, he had a very similar sense of humour to me and I felt safe to express my thoughts fully, without the worry of offending anyone.

It was not long before we were on a night shift and we were sent to a call that would end in my first ever arrest.

We were assigned a patch to patrol, one of the outer estates of the town known as Nacton and set about searching for crime or traffic offences to deal with, when the call came in.

When a member of public calls the police on 999, an emergency call operator would instantly patch you through to the force covering the geographical area for where the call was being made. You would then describe the incident to the police call taker who would create a log of the incident (CAD – Computer-aided dispatch) which the police incident dispatcher can see immediately.

The call would be graded dependant on the severity of the incident, Grade A – Emergency –Immediate Response, from the time of the call officers will attend within 15 minutes for urban areas, and 20 minutes for rural areas. Grade B – Priority Response, to attend as soon as possible. Grade C – Scheduled response, attendance within 24 hours, if an appointment is not appropriate[4]. Over the years the wording of the grading system changed, but essentially meant the same thing.

This particular call was for an assault in the street and both the suspect and victim were still at the scene. When we arrived, it was in a residential street and we were greeted by a middle-aged man with blood all over his face, he was shouting, swearing and gesticulating that another man, further up the road, had hit him with a golf club.

With this, we walked up the street towards the other male, who was also mouthing off, at this point another police vehicle arrived to assist. We found the younger man standing beside a car, and holding a golf club, my mind started racing and going through everything, *"assault, arrest, caution, what if he attacks us, what do I say…"* My tutor thankfully engaged the man in conversation in a manner he'd understand, it went something like, *"PUT THE FUCKING CLUB DOWN NOW!!"* and confronted by 4 officers he did as requested. He then briefly told us the two of them had been in an argument about something trivial and things had gotten out of hand, whilst standing there listening I could see there was blood on his feet.

We have an offence, a victim and a suspect, a weapon and DNA evidence, my tutor looks at me and gives me that look of *"arrest him then!"* With a real sense of nerves and apprehension, I said to him,

"I am arresting you on suspicion of assault occasioning actual bodily harm….." then cautioned him, *"you do not have to say anything, but it may harm your defence if you do not mention when questioned something which you may later rely on in court, anything you do say may be given in evidence."*

I must have looked like a complete newbie, all robotic and nervous! Now to handcuff him, my tutor took hold of one of his arms and informed him he was being cuffed, the man was fully compliant, thank god! I put the cuffs on him and then we took him off to custody. In the end a painless and easy arrest, that was my first one now out of the way. A good friend later in my career said something that I think is very true and goes hand in hand with policing, *"The anticipation is often worse than the application."*

The unbelievable thing to me as a new officer was they turned out to be father and son, I couldn't believe families behaved like this. The sheltered life I once had!!

It was really good working with my tutor, he was experienced, very similar to me and so easy to get along with. He was also one for a bit of humour at work, and at every opportunity he got! Which I think was needed, especially within a stressful job, known in policing as 'bants' and something the Chief Officers try to make 'illegal' within the workplace.

He would often try and catch me out, and I guess being very new into the force it wasn't that hard to get me…

Whilst on patrol on yet another night shift, we had a call for a commercial burglary at a warehouse, when we arrived he said: *"you wait by the door, and I'll go in."* So, I'm standing there at the doorway as he disappears into the darkness of the building, a minute or so later I hear him shouting and screaming at the top of his voice, there was also loads of banging and crashing. *"What on earth is going on? Is he being attacked?"* I thought. This sent me into a major adrenaline rush, with panic and fear of what was happening and what I will now face. I drew my baton (ASP) in preparation to clobber a baddie, and then heard him rushing to get out, he got to the door with his uniform all ruffled, and all out of breath he shouted, *"RUN!"* I am now in a serious stress, I turned and as I took my first couple of paces to get away, he stopped and laughed. The git! He got me on that one.

It wouldn't be long before he gave it his best efforts again. We were on a late shift and had been tasked to go to a different town's custody suite, to collect a detainee and transport him back to our own custody block. The journey gave him about 30 minutes to get me prepped for his next moment of stardom. All the way there, he kept telling me that I needed to watch this person carefully, *"he is dangerous, often assaults Police and is incredibly strong."*

Now, in a car when transporting someone, one officer would sit behind the driver (enabling a fast response to any medical issue the detainee may have whilst also preventing harm to the driver), with the detainee also in the rear alongside the officer. I was now worried I'd be getting attacked in the confines of a car! Brilliant!! It hadn't even crossed my mind that violent offenders actually went in a Police van (meat wagon).

We arrived at the custody suite and he obviously wasn't satisfied he'd done enough yet, so kept telling me to be ready and know where all of my safety equipment is in case I needed it. With my nerves now going through the roof and my heart almost beating out of my chest, the custody Sergeant (Sgt) went to get the detainee for us.

With this, my colleague started doing shoulder stretches and kept taking deep breaths in readiness for the detainees' arrival.

A few minutes later the Sgt walked back into the room and went straight behind his high solid wooden desk, *"well, where's the detainee?"* I'm thinking, then from behind the desk I see the skinniest and shortest Irish ex-jockey appear, making drunken jokes and being overly friendly as he walked towards us, my tutor was almost in tears with laughter and introduced me to a well-known local alcoholic, who, as it turned out, was as harmless as a mini marshmallow. I couldn't believe it, he got me again!

During my 10 week tutorship, I had a record of certain goals to achieve, it was called the Professional Development Portfolio (PDP), with things like, taking victim and witness statements, arresting of compliant and non-compliant offenders, issuing tickets for traffic violations, complete stop searches and the subsequent paperwork, input crimes to the database etc…I found these were easy to achieve working in a busy town and it didn't take long until I had completed the requirements for my 10-week tutorship.

One thing that did amaze me, was how many incidents one officer would have on their investigative workload at any one time, I would be steady at about 20 ongoing investigations at any one time and in a typical day I would try to take statements, make enquiries, do door knocking, make arrests and try to get on with my workload, all whilst attending about 10 different incoming incidents that then added to my workload as I was trying to get rid of some, it was relentless. Then there would be days we were on scene preservation duty for a murder or a rape, conducting constant observations of "vulnerable" detainees in their cells or at the hospital, all this meaning I would get nothing done on my workload. I was hoping this would get easier to manage as I gained more experience and independence in my role. I would be wrong! And is a common and founded complaint amongst local policing.

It was the funny things that made this very overbearing and already stressful job manageable, an example being;

There had been a rape, the suspect, a male, had been detained and was in our custody, my tutor and I had to do constant observations on him until a Dr had taken forensic samples from him, we did this to prevent him from removing/destroying any DNA and/or physical evidence.

When the Dr arrived, we took the detainee to the Dr's room where he was to lay on an examination table completely naked, so the Dr could take DNA swabs from certain areas!!

As he laid there the Dr walked in, a really tall, round black Nigerian man, he unpacked the sealed samples box containing swabs and sealable evidence packets etc... And then proceeded to put on his head what he must have thought was a white paper hat to prevent his hair from contaminating any samples taken, but was, in fact, a pair of massive white paper underpants for the detainee to cover his woohoo.

With these on his head, he then started to take the intimate swabs, and with the detainee looking terrified at the thought of this mad Dr touching him, I could not contain myself any longer, I was in utter tears with laughter, a complete mess, the kind of laughing when you know you should be quiet, but cannot stop, and to make it worse, I kept seeing my tutor's shoulders shaking as he tried to contain his laughter which would set me off again, I had to leave the room! We didn't have the heart to tell the Dr and let him just get on with it.

This 10 week tutor period was a real eye-opener into the world of policing, it made me realise what goes on and how much the police deal with and put up with that the public wouldn't even know goes on.

One real eye-opener for me personally, was my first call to a pub fight, it was a well-known druggy location so it became a regular occurrence and place for the Police to attend, but with this being my first time, I won't forget it. It made me really appreciate the fact police officers walk into danger and have to stop violence whereas before this job I and many members of the public would choose to make a hasty retreat.

We were on a late shift which was drawing to a close when we got a call about disorder at the pub. My tutor and I, along with a few others, made our way there and when we arrived there was a group of about 10-15 men fighting with poles and lumps of wood in the carpark, as we stopped my tutor jumped out of the car and ran into it. *"Bloody hell! Here we go then!"* I thought. I got out and approached one of the men, he was shouting, swearing, bouncing about and showing real aggression towards me, I was trying my hardest to calm him down, but words were not doing anything. We were frightfully outnumbered and whilst trying to push people apart, I heard this almighty and really powerful siren getting closer and then stopping right behind me, another police car had just pulled up right behind us, it was a Roads Policing Unit, which had come into the town to help us out. The Roads Policing Officer and I then literally had to bundle the bloke to the floor and amidst him trying to kick and punch us both we somehow managed to handcuff him and got him away to a police van.

In what seemed like 10 long minutes, but was probably only 1 or 2, order had been restored. Then it would be back to the station to write statements and prepare a handover for the night shift to deal with all those that had been arrested. I remember that this incident made me incredibly late off and only gave me about 9 hours before my next shift was scheduled to start.

During the early stages of a career, new recruits had to go on attachments with other departments, one week with each, the Roads Policing Unit (RPU), Criminal Investigation Department (CID), Prisoner handling and Scenes of Crime. Only the RPU one got me excited, so when that came up I was really pleased. I spent one week with the RPU officers, they had bigger and faster cars, more independence with the whole county to Police, and, through my observation, were considerably more respected by the public and other emergency services.

During my time with them, we (they, I observed) patrolled the major roads, dealt with the more serious collisions, targeted the more serious offenders using vehicles, and also wrote up varying tickets for vehicle-related offences such as speeding, using a phone, construction and use violations, the list goes on…. It confirmed to me that this was going to be my path if I can achieve it, I first have to complete 2 years general patrol before any specialisms were allowed.

I thankfully managed to dodge the CID one, it never interested me, they conduct the investigation into the more serious crime such as rape, residential burglary, large scale fraud and also murder, but it was often seen as a dept. of statement writing and very little action, which would have bored me to tears, being an office junky.

The patrol officer would generally deal with the initial scenes for all of those incidents and then be tasked with the arrests. CID conducted the slow time investigation and took the statements! And lots of them. I dare say there was a lot more to it than that, but it didn't float my boat and I take my hat off to those that do, as the investigations were much more complex than I wanted at the moment, I wanted real-time, quick moving, action and adventure.

So, when my turn came, it was a requirement to wear a suit, NO! I hate them remember! Well, I told the supervisor I will not be buying a new suit for a role I do not want in the future and luckily he didn't want to waste my time either, so win-win.

My prisoner processing attachment got delayed due to staffing issues for over a year so I didn't mind that either. This dept. was at that time staffed with warranted officers on long term sick/injured and civilian support staff, it was created with the intention that when an officer made an arrest for a crime, had gained statements and captured any other available evidence, the prisoner processing unit would then take on the interview and any subsequent file preparation for the courts. The reality was very much different, mainly due to staffing, they would only have the capacity to take on a few jobs a day so it was not anywhere near enough to keep an entire team of officers on the street.

My 10 weeks tutor period came to an end towards the end of October 2005 and I would now be classed as 'ready for independent patrol,' ready to go it alone.
Until my driving course though, I would have to be double crewed with other officers on my shift.

I, and my other new colleagues, luckily didn't have long to wait and my driving course was due to start at the end of November 2005. I love driving, I love cars and I love speed, so I was mega excited to learn to drive, Police style!

Now, in the British Police there are a number of driving courses available;

- The A to B ticket – This was a 2-3 day course used for civilian employees and Special Constables (volunteer warranted officers), to enable them to drive Police owned vehicles from one location to another, adhering to all traffic regulations, merely a mode of transport. They could use the blue lights to request a motorist to stop or guard a scene, but, the driver was not authorised to pursue any fleeing motorist, and had no exemptions to the law.

- The Standard Response course – This was a 3-week course for employed, warranted officers of the Constabulary and select Special Constables. Using low to mid powered marked vehicles to respond to emergencies and being allowed certain exemptions of the Road Traffic Act; Speed limits, Red Stop lights & keep left bollards to assist in a quick response to incidents and enable Police officers to productively do their job. It is a commonly mistaken belief amongst the public, and to correct you I shall say this; The British Police, DO NOT have to have their blue lights and/or siren on to use the exemptions. This course would authorise the driver to pursue a fleeing vehicle in the initial phase of a pursuit, but only if a full pursuit trained Roads Policing Officer was available, and could readily take over command of the pursuit. A refresher course would be held every 5 years and would be 1 week in length.

- The 4x4 Course – This was for those who had completed the Standard Response course and, had a need to use low-mid powered Four Wheel Drive vehicles to respond to incidents with the same exemptions and to use the vehicle off-road.
- The Advanced Driving Course – This was a 4-week course for those who had successfully completed the Standard Response course to a higher standard and, were specialising into a Dept. where the use of high-performance vehicles was needed such as, Roads Policing, Firearms & Surveillance. This was an access all areas course, do this and drive anything. A refresher course would be held every 3 years and would be 1 week in length. Failure of the refresher resulted in the advanced driver status being returned to the standard category.
- The Pursuit course – This was a 1 week course for those who had successfully completed both the Standard Response Course & the Advanced Driving Course, it would enable the driver to be a Commander for vehicle pursuits and to make

command decisions on which tactics to use, and to implement those tactics to stop the fleeing vehicle. It was not rank specific and being a pursuit commander gave you the control over the tactical options of an authorised Police pursuit. This was refreshed every 3 years, again 1 week in length.

Late November 2005 I started my Standard Response Course, it was cold, frosty and icy. As an eager beaver, I was there for day one bright and early, and as is the norm with probably every occupational training course it started with the usual administration of the course, and a round robin of who we are and where we're based. I hated the whole introducing yourself shindig, the *"Hi I'm Jerry and I'm an alcoholic"* joke, wouldn't go down well in this environment, but I knew greater things were to come. It did give me one laugh though, one of the instructors, whom I would become good friends with during my career, was talking to us about the "limit point" when cornering, and whilst doing so went to sit casually on the edge of a table, which then broke and went crashing to the ground, taking him with it! Bloody hilarious! It killed me… The look on someone's face, at that very moment they know they are going to fall, gets me every time.

We were given what would become our driving bibles, the handbook entitled "Road Craft, the Police driver's handbook." During this 3 week course, I must have read it back to back 2-3 times, and I hate reading! But loved this, this is my kind of porn!

We were divided up into three groups of three and assigned a training vehicle, mine was a year 2000 Ford Mondeo, with a 2.0-litre engine, going 0-62mph in somewhere around 8-9 seconds, it was front wheel driven and had a 5-speed manual gearbox. Not the quickest machine in the world but still enabled us to have good fun.

We were then introduced to our instructor (a qualified Police Advanced Driver, with a driver training certification) who would be with us for the duration of the course.

At the start of every day, the vehicles must be clean, fuelled, had oil & fluids checked, tyres checked for pressure and wear, windscreen wipers and washer fluid checked and all lights and the horn checked.

A few things had to happen on this course that I didn't like! First off was a cockpit drill, this was a spoken script of things you've checked on the car before driving off, and then on the road, we would do a few minutes commentary on what we were seeing, doing, anticipating etc… All of this was intended to show the instructor what we are thinking as we do things, to show what we are mentally processing and as a way to learn to do it properly, after all, we will be driving at warp 9 so things had to be right!

The Cockpit drill was pretty much like this, if my memory is right; *"My handbrake is on and my gear lever is in neutral, my seat and mirrors are adjusted to my liking, my door is closed and my seatbelt is on, could passengers please check theirs. Turning the ignition key to the first stage, I am greeted by an array of warning lights, most of which extinguish after a self-test period. With the clutch depressed and the footbrake brake firmly applied I am starting the engine, noting the final warning lights now go out. The engine temperature is in the normal range and I have sufficient fuel for my journey. Checking in my mirrors along the body of the car I can see the doors and fuel flap are all shut. Selecting first gear, checking all around including any blind spots and releasing the parking brake I can now safely move off."*

We would then make our way out of the Headquarters complex and perform a brake test on the long driveway. *"I am about to perform a brake test. Applying the footbrake firmly the vehicle pulls up to a controlled stop with no adverse effects felt on the steering."*

We started off slow and had to drive the instructor around the town and some local rural roads, at normal speeds and obeying all laws, this would give him our base standard to work from. I was so pleased I had done that civilian advanced driving course before the Police, I was instantly top of the class, a place I liked being!! Who doesn't if they're honest?

Then as the day(s) progressed so did our speeds, we would be driving the rural routes passing everything we came across, I should point out this was all done in an unmarked vehicle without blue lights activated, so to members of the public we were just any other public vehicle, but thrashing along! I loved it, I loved the feeling of being behind another car, entering a bend in the correct position, speed and gear and then as soon as a view appeared we were out, check for hidden junctions or hazards and then pass them, then on to the next one.

It continued like that for the rest of the course, it was mentally shattering mind you, each night I would sleep like a baby.

Whilst on the road our instructor would choose a moment that we had to do our moving commentary, at times it was when driving normal speeds and also when at high speeds, as I've said, the instructor cannot see in your head at what you are seeing, thinking, anticipating and planning so this gave him that chance.

As an example it would go something like this; *"Today I am driving a Ford Mondeo 5 speed manual, the roads are dry, the traffic is light and the weather is overcast. I am currently on the A1066 heading towards the town of Thetford. My current speed is 90mph. The road ahead is twisty and lined by a high thick hedge, looking at the telegraph poles I can anticipate the direction of the upcoming turns. I can see a junction ahead on my right which is clear of traffic and I am gaining on a vehicle ahead which is going at a much slower pace, looking beyond the vehicle I can see the road turns sharply to the right, I plan to overtake if safe as we exit that bend, as we approach the bend I am moving up into a contact position and have tucked myself against the verge allowing for a quicker view exiting the bend, I have slowed sufficiently and chosen the correct gear to allow rapid acceleration. Looking through the bend I can see no oncoming traffic and the road straightens out. Exiting the bend, checking my side mirror and moving out, the road ahead is clear, now accelerating past the vehicle I can see an upcoming left-hand bend, remaining on this side of the road affords me a greater view into the left-handed bend, but ensuring to be on the correct side of the road before the limit point."*

As the course went on we also spent some time on the skid pan, learning to control the car in spins (most of the time!) and to experience the loss of traction under different situations, enabling us to gauge when the traction broke and then how to correct it. I remember two very distinct incidents during the driving course;

1) We were driving on roads in the open country, the roads were elevated above the surrounding flat fields and views went on for miles all around. I was rapidly gaining on a Tractor that was too wide to pass, I saw a small single vehicle width track that left the road to the left, it went down a dip and back up joining the same road again about 200 yards ahead, I timed my arrival to the tractor with that of the access track, I shot down it and re-joined the road

ahead of the tractor, the instructor loved it! A spot of improvised rally intertwined with the course. Brilliant.

2) I was driving some very bendy roads with fast long straights between them in a forestry area, ahead I saw I was gaining on another car, this one was from the same course as us, and in my mind, I knew what I would have to do, *"I am having him!"* I thought. I was nailing the bends and was flat out along the straights, reeling him in each time, I caught him up, entered a bend directly behind him, tucked the car right up behind him, got my view and I was out, it was all clear and I floored it, I smashed him to pieces down the straight and disappeared through the next few bends. It was bloody brilliant!!!! I was buzzing, as were my colleagues in the car, the instructor did say that doesn't normally happen, which made me feel even better.

The next day, the driver of that other car, at the time I had passed it, had apparently complained to the lead instructor that I had ruined his drive by overtaking him, and it had affected his confidence, I mean honestly! From that point on, the training cars never went the same routes as each other again. That rule continued for my whole career.

We then spent some time using the blue lights and sirens both in the towns and on the rural routes before the final test day came. We had a written exam on road traffic signs and legislation, then the in-car assessment by the lead instructor. I passed comfortably with a recommendation that I do the advanced driving course in the future, this also meant I could now go out on my own in a police car and respond to incidents.

I returned to my base station, and my car was a 2004 fully marked Ford Focus estate, with a 1.8 TDCI engine, it was not at all powerful doing 0-62mph in a pitiful 9-10 seconds and could only get up to about 110-115 mph if you had the space, and it took a while getting there! But, I was still pleased as punch, the rest of the team must have loved me too, because from then on whenever a job came in, I was going. Crash, domestic, assault, theft, you name it, I wanted to drive about with my lights going, this was now my perfect world, other than the now ever-growing workload from being so keen!!

 As I had already decided I wanted to go down the Roads Policing route, I started to attend as many collisions as possible and deal with as many motoring offences as I could find. The problem being, in the busy environment of this town, I did not get that much spare time to be proactive, so I was unable to build much, good quality evidence for any application in the future.

 I therefore decided to concentrate on getting through my first 2 years and go from there, and I very quickly learnt that my eagerness caused others to become extremely lazy. An example was a day I had been responding to most jobs, no help or word from others and didn't get a lunch or even decent drinks break. The shift was coming to an end and I had quite a few crimes to input when I got back to the station before leaving off. When I got back I found the rest of my shift already in the office playing card games, I was not happy and told them as much!

 My 1st year on patrol continued with the ever-increasing demand of workload investigations and the growing number of real-time incidents requiring attendance, it was a common occurrence to be late off, so much so that being off on time was actually the rare event.

 Overtime was paid to you the following month or you could bank it and take the time due, the first 30 minutes, however, was not claimable as a payment due to a historic agreement on police pay. Annoyingly, the norm was being 30-40 minutes late off so you tended to just lose your own time.

I know it doesn't seem much, but when you consider you were in early to be kitted, prepped and ready to be out the door for an incident at your actual start time, not just to turn up at the start time, as is the case in many work environments, then, during the shift it was common to have no time for a lunch break and to attend violent assaults, suicides, sudden deaths, crashes and domestic abuse calls etc. etc. it was very mentally draining and going home time was so very much needed. Would you honestly want in your time of need an exhausted and unfocused officer turning up to help? I wouldn't!

Within the 1st year a few jobs stuck in my mind for differing reasons. One such an incident, like this one, was a feeling of doing my job well and also experiencing the frustration of trying, but not being able to help someone, who very clearly needed it;

I was dispatched to attend a nearby park where a 20 something-year-old female had been found by a member of the public, with dirt all over her and a number of minor injuries. It was a very dark evening, and when I arrived, I found the female who was very upset. She identified herself to me by name, but due to the dark, I could only make out she had blonde hair, a pinkish top and blue jeans. I decided to take her back to her address so I could ask her in the comfort of her own home about what had happened with her that evening, and why someone would call the Police about her.

During our short journey, she only spoke briefly and very quietly. I learnt that she had been with a man for about 7 months and had been living with him for the last couple of weeks. She told me that in the past, this man had been verbally abusive to her and was trying to control every aspect of her life, she also said that he had even broken the bathroom lock when she was inside. A line that is very true to a lot of people *"you don't really know someone until you live with them"* was expressed. I was told her partner lost control this night and she didn't want him in any trouble, and that was it, she then stopped talking.

We got to her address and I went inside, nobody else was there, the female followed me in also. This was the 1st time I had seen her in full light, she had long dark mascara streaks running down her cheeks and she looked fragile and scared, she was still very quietly spoken, even in the house. She had grass stains on the knees of her jeans and forearms of her top. She presented as someone who was worried about a very real threat to her.

As a Police Officer, in the ideal world, you should be able to detach from emotion to assist you in your job and avoid personal views getting in the way of evidence gathering. I was still new and am not afraid to say I felt very sorry for her, she was a broken woman and needed my help.

After a short while, I made her a tea and tried to find out what had happened. She initially spoke again and told me that her partner and she had been out for a drink in a local pub, and on the walk home her partner had suggested they go through the park, she didn't know why he wanted to but they did. She then said that she had fallen over in the park and then she completely totally stopped talking again, refusing to say anything further. I saw a cut on her right hand and the base of her chin, she must have noticed me look at the hand because she very quickly covered it up. She briefly started to talk to me about other things that in no way related to this incident and never spoke of this night's events again.

For no apparent reason her character quickly changed, she became panicky and fidgety and then she told me to leave, I had no choice and had to. I left there feeling as though I had left somebody who needs real help but my hands were tied, I was not happy about that, so I would at least try….

I passed her information on to other agencies who deal with domestic violence and also approached the Crown prosecutors for their opinion. There was nothing more I could do, she wouldn't talk to me and without any evidence, the prosecutors couldn't do anything, and after all, she had apparently *"fallen over!"* There were no cameras to capture anything, the caller didn't see anything other than the lady in the same state I found her, and no houses overlooked the area.

To this day, I know there was a lot she never told me, I hope I at least showed her people can and are willing to help and that she managed to find some help. I never heard of or saw her again.

A few days later, my supervisor and also the Constabulary training manager wanted a meeting with me about this incident, again, as a new cop, I thought it was for a yelling at, but was, in fact, the very opposite, they had heard from somewhere, but didn't tell me where, that I had tried to help with this lady even after being told to leave and I had tried hard to get some form of presentable evidence, they said a lot of experienced officers would have left it there at her house, but that my approach was correct and more people should be like that. Was it her? The prosecutors? Outside agencies? I don't know, but at least I made an impression on someone.

Then there were the instances where people made an impression on me, sadly and if I'm honest, the vast majority of people I came across when working in the town, left me with an impression that a section of public was either incompetent at solving even the slightest of their of own problems, or they would make me take a strong disliking towards them, often it was through their actions towards others, whether it was an utter lack of respect for the Police or more often than not a total disregard for the property of others.

In this example you will see that when younger groups got together "with nothing to do!" they turned feral, causing trouble for anyone and everyone, not realising or more likely, not caring that people then have to sort out the mess they leave in their wake. It also highlighted to me early on in my career, that Police officers often attend incidents not knowing if they will come away from it without harm, they have to approach situations that other people can walk or run away from.

I know it's their job, but, could you walk up to someone brandishing knives or other weapons and threatening to harm you if you go over to them, bearing in mind at this time of my career, Police only had handcuffs, a baton and CS spray (which affects everyone, including the user!). Add into the mix that you have been up all night, going from one job to the next, you are utterly shattered and just want to get home?

Most people I know after a few hours of driving when just going on vacation want a break at the end of it, not to jump straight into another violent or traumatic incident like the emergency services do daily.

So, you are at home getting ready for work, it is early in the morning and looking outside you see a group of feral kids… Is this acceptable as something to do, just because?

In July 2006, my shift had been on nights, we had been busy as usual, flying around the town dealing with, drunks, domestics, burglaries and scuffles here and there, the norm for nights… There were 15 minutes until we got to turn our radios off and go home.

We were all back at the station waiting for the day shift to kit up and take over… *"damn it! A call!!" "Three males in a residential street walking up and down kicking cars and breaking the mirrors and wipers off."* On the face of it, not too serious. It was only a couple of minutes away so the area car attended and within seconds of their arrival, their emergency button had been activated.

The Police digital radios had a function called the emergency button, press it and it cuts off traffic from all other radios on your talk-group and gives you an open microphone and priority over other users, usually a feature reserved for the incident dispatchers. Everyone can then hear what the radio user has going on. With the sound of a lot of shouting, commotion and loud commands from the officers *"GET BACK!"* We knew it was more serious than first thought. Should it be needed the Police vehicle and personal radios also had a pinpoint location tracker built in.

I was double crewed for the shift, driving obviously! It helps when your colleague hates driving. Fine with me! We and another car attended to assist. Arriving first we immediately saw the two officers from the area car standing back to back with batons drawn and raised, shouting around them in a circle was a group of, as it turned out, 15 people all aged 15/16 yrs. old, and, all with wooden clubs or metal poles swinging for the two officers. Even with us attending it was still a very uneven fight! (As is the daily life of the Police, they have to make very quick real-time decisions, often to the complaint of the armchair cops who analyse in slow time what they do!). I knew we wouldn't be able to do much on our own, *"what can I do? I know!"* As I approached I put my siren on to the loudest, fastest note possible, the sound to all outside and near to it would be a deafening, screeching white noise, I had decided I would drive at the group of feral little shits.

With the officers at great risk of serious injury, even with us there, the gloves were off! I drove at them as I arrived with the intention to take as many as possible out in one hit, I ploughed through the group like a train hitting a snow pile, well that moved them! Bloody impressively too! Even if I do say so myself. With a few knocked in to touch, that had evened things up a bit and with the other police cars now arriving, we issued out some knee strikes, pushes, sprays, baton strikes, hits and also getting hit and the group was reduced to a heap on the floor and were duly arrested.

The unfortunate side to this was then conveying them to custody and getting them booked in and searched (which can take about 30 minutes per person), complete our own statements and compile a handover report for the day turn to process them, it was late off again! And properly! That little incident left me with a swollen and reddened hand, and hindered the movement of my fingers – that was from being whacked, and my back was sore at the base of my spine.

Police are often criticised for using force, or as often publicised "excessive" force, having been on the side of the Police I can honestly say that force is sometimes needed, whether the public agree with it or not, in this instance, if force had not been used, then every cop would most likely have taken a good clubbing, the group would then go on, doing more damage, causing misery for local residents and then hurting the public if they tried to stop them. Police officers believe it or not don't actually want to use force on anyone! It'd be great if they could say *"Stop doing that"* and people did just stop without any qualms. Sadly this is not always the case. Would you have used force in this scenario? You may agree or disagree with how it was dealt with but at the very end of the day, it wasn't you having to make that very quick decision, and I standby the opinion that if someone is prepared to attack the Police when exercising their lawful duty to keep others safe and their property undamaged, the Police should respond and robustly!

The robust approach was also very welcomed when it was dished out by the courts! Unfortunately, not very often I think most of you will agree! Still in my first 2 years, I managed to get a few people into Jail for reasonably good stretches given the offences, two of which were for very different offences! And I was doing what I thought the police should be doing, putting people behind bars.

Still In the summer of 2006, I was patrolling the outlying housing estates, this particular estate was well known for high volumes of vehicle crime and the cover-all offence for a lot of the local residents of, being a *"dick!"* I was following a Doctors response car along a 30 mph residential road when I saw a motorcycle pull out of a side street directly in front of the Dr's car. It then proceeded to pull away at quite a lick. I passed the Dr's car and matched the pace of the motorbike, about 70-80mph, in a 30! Knowing I was not a Roads Policing Officer and not pursuit tactics authorised I decided to prevent a pursuit from happening, he didn't know I was there yet and was completely unaware of my presence. I passed him and pulled straight across the front of him, forcing him to an abrupt stop, bikes can't reverse very easily so job done. The rider dropped the bike and then ran for it. A sign of guilt if ever I've seen one!

Now, I do not like running after people, wearing all the Police clobber doesn't make for an easy 100-metre sprint compared to someone wearing a tracksuit and trainers! So I chose to trip him up. With him now rolling to a stop I got some cuffs on him pretty quick and I saw he was wearing a tag on his leg (court imposed for monitoring and enforcing curfews).

I found out who he was and it was revealed he had outstanding warrants for numerous burglaries, assaults, frauds, traffic offences – being disqualified amongst them, drug offences and now whatever I could find. On checking the bikes license plate I found he had adapted one of the letters with tape to resemble a different letter, and there was also the initial speeding offence to add to his list.

He was arrested, charged and then sentenced, much to my disbelief he got 8 years in prison for all of the offences combined. I couldn't believe it!! Good job done I thought. I received a well done by senior ranks of the station and I was left feeling very chuffed with myself. And to the members of the public who say the Police should catch burglars instead of speeders, well this started out as "just a speeder" and as often happens, it snowballs from there!

Burglars don't wear black and white striped tops and carry swag bags like in the old cartoons, it may surprise some people but they look like any other person. I always said to people when they moaned, *"Well, you point one out to me and I will catch them!"*

Staying with me not wanting to get into foot chases… I'll quickly drop this one in before we get back to my next imprisonment…bear with me!

I had been called to an address where a 16yr old kid had smashed the front window of someone's house, as I turned up I parked around the corner so I could walk around and catch him completely unaware. As I rounded the corner I saw this really dumpy kid hurling abuse at the residents of the damaged house, and as I got closer behind him and almost within reach, he realised I was there and went to run, well waddle! Not even you mate! I am not chasing people on foot!!!!! I swung out my leg hooking his trailing foot and he fell like a rock, rebounded a touch and rolled to a stop. Sorry, that one made me laugh at the time!
Back to the prison people…

The next, and not quite so glamorous arrest, but as the year would develop it may well have saved this person's life!

On a hot summer's day a small convenience store in an area known locally as "mini Europe," due to the high volume of the different nationalities of Eastern Europeans living there, reported a theft. I attended to take the theft report as is normal, and it transpired the offender had stolen a single packet of Jaffa Cakes! Hmmm, the diverse array of offences I got to deal with! For the shop owner mind you, this was becoming a regular occurrence – thefts that is. So to him, it was serious. I took the report using my best acting skills to feign some sort of interest in this very low-level crime, and then top it off he knew who the offender was and had video evidence too, now I really do have to deal with it!

I was told the person's name and it was someone already well known to me, a female, drug using prostitute, and she had once even propositioned me when walking back from work one late evening, I obviously turned her down! Even with the "Police discount!"

With all the relevant evidence captured I conducted a check and found out she was on prison recall (released from prison on the proviso she does not commit a crime in a certain time frame, or she'd have to return and complete the full sentence, with any new sentence on top).

Off I trotted with a colleague to her last known address and once there, I started knocking on the door and we were told to go away, or as she put it *"FUCK OFF!"* So, we now knew she was inside and force was used to enter. It was an apartment in a block made up of dingy flats, the apartment itself stank of awfully bad hygiene, smoke, dirt and faeces (human and animal). It's very hard to explain exactly, it was just skanky! And dark.

We located her in her bedroom and could see empty alcoholic bottles scattered everywhere, clothes all over the place, cigarette butts in anything that would hold them and there she was, lying naked on her bed with a scummy stained sheet underneath her, shouting and gesticulating at us. I told her numerous times to get up, put some clothes on and that she was coming with us. Well, she wasn't having any of it! Brilliant! Now I had to fight with her on the bed, oh joy! Cutting a vile story short, we managed to grab her and mummify her in the disgusting sheet, bag some clothes and then with some forceful persuasion she put a few items on. She was arrested and taken to custody where I interviewed her for the theft and charged her.

Owing to the prison recall stipulation, she was then sent to prison for the remaining 2 years of her sentence. A nice result from a stolen packet Jaffa cakes I thought!

One major problem with arresting drug addicts was something that had to be done, but was not very nice following the arrest, the strip search! Male officers searched males and females searched female, for obvious reasons!

The sight of a malnourished and scrawny body with various miscellaneous rashes all over them and the smell of month old damp sweaty socks and dirty arse crack would be impregnated in their clothes and skin. This was not a nice job, I know it wasn't nice for them either and must have truly been very embarrassing for them, but I don't give a damn, it was me having to look at them!

Despite this we did try to do it with some dignity, they would be stripped to just their underpants and t-shirt, examining all the clothing as it came off, with gloves and a blocked nose! How socks get that wet I don't know! Then the t-shirt would be removed, arms raised and the person made to do a 360-degree turn. T-shirt back on, underpants off, first a 360 turn holding their t-shirt up to the chest, then with them facing you, they would be instructed to lift their woohoo out of the way and then the testicular sack! Next, they would turn away from you and bend forward at 90 degrees, they would be told to open their butt cheeks... Fucking disgusting! If all was clear, clothes were thrown back at them and then they would be taken to their cell. Copious amounts of alcohol hand gel would then be rubbed in all over my hands and arms, it was just a pity you couldn't rub it in your eyes too!

With all of these incidents I and my team were getting involved in on a daily basis, the workloads would grow bigger and bigger, to counter that, there were certain jobs people would rush to volunteer for because it did not involve any further work once dealt with at the scene, these were mainly Sudden Deaths.

A sudden death was when a person died unexpectedly and/or had not seen a Dr in the previous 14 days in-relation to an ongoing illness, these would range from the elderly in a care home, to bad smells near, or at a property that led to the discovery of a dead body and also the people who died in a public place.

Police would attend under the power of, and as an official representative of the coroner to deal with the death and have the body removed for any following investigation, including an autopsy.

I attended a lot of these in my 4 years working in the town of Ipswich (roughly 100), and in most of the circumstances that you could possibly imagine, the elderly in a care home, cardiac arrest in the street, various types of suicide, the Emergency Dept. at the hospital, being hit by a train and being found floating in a river. A few would stick in my mind for varying reasons; Apologies now if you're squeamish!

One morning, a call came in from a young boy who had found his mother lying face down on the floor of her bedroom and was not responding.

Upon attending this one, the front door was locked and force was used to enter the property. A young boy was found distressed inside, he was left downstairs with an officer whilst I and another went upstairs. In the main bedroom, we found a young lady laid on her front next to the bed, but on the floor. A clear plastic tube ran from an empty oxygen tank down and under her face, her hands were up by her head and she was wearing night clothes.

She was very cold to the touch and her body was rigid with rigour mortis, we rolled her over and could see her face was flattened and purple from the pooling blood and dead weight, the oxygen mask was stuck to her mouth and her stomach although flattened still had a slight bulge, she was heavily pregnant. An ambulance arrived almost straight away and the on-board paramedic confirmed what we already knew, the pregnant mother of the little boy was dead. It was a very saddening set of circumstances.

We searched the property and found contact details for some relatives, but before a Police Officer could attend their address to inform them, some of the local residents upon seeing the police and ambulance activity must have contacted them first, it was not long before we had the ladies' parents at the address and inconsolable with the news we then gave them.

A call to an address by a neighbour, stating a house stank and the occupant, a single elderly man, had not been seen for some time.

I attended this address confident it would be a death from the information given on the call. I arrived and could see flies had filled the window panes at the front of the house, and the smell of death was very clear near the property and much stronger through the doors mailbox, again force was used to enter. The smell of death and decomposing human remains was gut-wrenching, it was very hot inside and the smell had rushed out the front door like it was trying to escape from what was inside, blanketing me in the fog of it all.

I started the search for what I knew was going to be a dead body. I went door by door until I was left with the living room, this door was shut and the smell coming from behind it permeated through the cracks. I knew this was the door and even when you've found loads of bodies before, the feeling of anticipation and that shock factor still fills your body, it is truly a strange feeling.

As I opened the door, another blast of hot air filled with the heavy scent of decay knocked me back, taking a second to catch my breath (although not too deep) I walked through the doorway into what was a small living room, with a small table, a couple of armchairs, and there on the floor was the body of an elderly man, hunched down on his knees in a kneeling foetal/praying position, wearing only a pair of underpants.

There was a large wet ring around him visible in the carpet, where his bodily fluids had over time been running out and then been soaked up. Half of his body had decomposed so badly that it had only left a jelly-like goo on the bones. His forehead was rested on the floor and most of the skull had been exposed, except on the back of his head. The problem here was he had died (and some time ago) in front of a bar heater that was still glowing red hot, it had literally slowly cooked and melted him. *"The poor old boy, what a way to be found I thought!"* It is very true that death does not have any dignity and it often comes at an inconvenient time. I didn't need an ambulance this time, it was clear he was gone.

The coroner's service was then called to take the man to the mortuary, and the icing on the cake was when we tried lifting him up to put him into a body bag, the rest of any remaining flesh just fell off, it was utterly disgusting.

I searched for any contact details that could be for friends or family but found none and speaking to a neighbour, it was apparent he kept to himself and never had visitors, it was believed he was completely alone.

Even in the face of such a horrible scene, it was still very sad that this person who would have had a life full of stories of his own to tell, would be able to die and nobody was in his life to know it had happened, until he was found in this state and only then because of the smell.

That night when I got home to my partner, I was told to have a shower immediately, I apparently stunk, and to think I'd been to several other incidents during that day, but I must have gotten so used to the smell I didn't realise.

Sudden deaths calls would always throw something up just to keep you on your toes, this one example literally nearly killed me!

One night shift, I was dispatched to attend an address on the outskirts of the town, another elderly man lived there all alone. His family, who lived at the other end of the country had not heard from him for days and he would not answer his phone, so there was a genuine concern for his welfare.

I arrived at the semi-rural address, which was set in amongst some large pine trees, it was a very dark night and the lights to the house were all off. I started off by banging on the doors and windows, *"Police, Open your door!"* I did this for about 10 minutes but to no avail. I then asked The Police control room to call the registered phone for that address, hoping he'll answer it and be told to get to the door.

I heard it ringing and ringing and ringing, but it never got answered! Whilst checking the doors and windows I found that the back patio door had been left unlocked. I took out my torch and entered the house, again going from room to room flicking the light switches on as I went, and calling out; *"Police, respond to me!"* but nobody was replying.

The house was relatively tidy and did not smell at all. I continued to search and downstairs was empty, I then went upstairs, still calling out; *"It's the Police!"* and still got no response. I opened up the bedroom doors and finally opened one and found an elderly man lying on his back motionless with his mouth open and silent on the bed. I called out again and still got no reply, a confirmed death I thought. With my light beaming on his face I walked up to him, and as I reached out and took hold of his shoulder, he screamed out *"AHHHHHH!"* really loudly and launched himself sideways with such a start it made my heart pound like a bolt of lightning had just struck me, I may have also made an involuntary sound myself, perhaps at both ends, who knows!!

Once he'd calmed down, it turned out he was as deaf as post and had not replaced the batteries in his hearing aid for the last few days, until then, after I had met him. With the family updated by a call, I went on my merry way to whatever society had to throw at me next.

One other Sudden death that I will remember, again for a completely different reason, was the call to an address, also as a concern for welfare, but this time from a distant friend.

It was the search of the property following his discovery that I remember this time. As is normal in these circumstances, a search for details of close relatives would be undertaken, the problem now, was this house was cluttered like heck. The floors had stepping stone type spaces amongst the clutter of bags, boxes and fabrics, you name it, and it was there, making piles from the floor to ceiling, a very obvious lifelong hoarder.

Well, my colleague and I started to look here and there and we found no contact details for anyone whatsoever, we did find a last will and testament declaring the entirety of his estate was to be given to a care home that helps those in the advanced stages of cancer.

As we looked through the drawers, we kept finding envelopes with notes of money in them, one after the other and everywhere we looked, we kept finding them. Due to the house now going to be empty and no relatives immediately available, it was decided we should collect up any money that is easily found for safe keeping in the Constabulary vault, until a solicitor for the gentleman gets involved to settle his estate, rather than now leave it to be burgled by some low-life criminal who finds out the place is empty.

We got some serialised property bags and started to collect the money up and we asked for a supervisor to be present to oversee this so no accusations could be made against us! After a while, we had checked the immediately accessible areas and had totalled £55,000 or about $100,000 of cash, and there was bound to be more hidden away. The friend had been notified and it transpired the gentleman owned his house without a mortgage and kept all of his money in his house as he didn't trust the banks to look after it, it's a good job he never got burgled or he would have lost everything.

Attending a number of Sudden deaths and seeing the people's bodies being "tagged & bagged" grew my interest in an often closed procedure, the autopsy.

After making contact with the local morticians I had arranged to watch over a post mortem. I arrived bright-eyed and full of interest, it's something most of us have seen on TV and now I was seeing it done first hand. With an apron on and a really friendly female pathologist as my guide, I watched intently and took the opportunity to ask as many questions as I could.

She started to open up an elderly lady and explained all the internal parts and what she was looking for as she went. It was not at all like the TV shows depict with really wet bloody organs, and hands and arms getting soaked in blood. It was in fact very clean. Yes, there was some blood, but due to the body having died and then been laid on the back for a while, all the blood had pooled along the back of the body cavity removing it from most of the organ and muscle tissues.

After the chest, stomach and bowels, she moved on to removing the tongue by cutting the neck open and pulling it out through the throat, she then sliced it like a ham looking for any signs of disease. With that done she proceeded to skin the top of the head, and shortly afterwards out came the high pitched mini circular saw, and within seconds she had cut the top of the skull, pried it off and removed the brain, chopping and dicing looking for any tell-tale signs of problems.

The body was put back together and the final conclusion was death as a result of complications from pneumonia. A very interesting experience and one I was glad to have witnessed. I would not feel the same mind you when I returned some years later for a 1-year-old child!

It was this experience of seeing the investigation into the death of a person and how every part of that person formed the final conclusion that led me to volunteer for some additional training, I would become trained for mass disaster body recovery, but I'm pleased to tell you, I never had to do it.

Late 2006, the town of Ipswich in Suffolk saw what would become one of the UK's most prolific serial killings of modern times. The red light area of Ipswich was as active as usual, it was very common to see ladies working as prostitutes on a number of the town centre streets.

I was working my usual shifts of days, lates and nights, and during this time one of the local prostitutes was reported as missing and not seen or heard from. It is an unfortunate truth for the ladies that get into prostitution that they are always at high risk of incident, they would often get into a strangers car, and go to dark hidden away areas to serve their client in a bid to avoid the Police finding them or their client.

A report was taken by an officer, as is the case for any missing person, but I was not part of it at this stage so it would be wrong to comment on any of the investigations.

A couple of weeks later with the 1st lady still missing, a second lady, also a known prostitute was reported missing too. There was a very evident change to me that the Constabulary not only changed gear but turned all concentration to finding them, the force diverted many resources to do house to house enquiries, giving out missing person pamphlets at a football game and followed up on any and every report of female belongings being found, people screaming, alarms going off, you name it we checked it.

A couple of weeks after that, a body of a young lady had been found in a brook near some fishing lakes just outside of the town, the general consensus amongst the frontline patrol officers was that it was going to be one of the two missing ladies, and it sure enough it was. A large cordoned off area was set up and officers were posted all over to prevent the media, and public from hindering in the recovery of evidence. It was a really cold December and I can remember sitting in a Police mobile hut at the scene absolutely freezing on constant watch for anyone testing the cordon.

The next two days saw a further two ladies go missing, again known prostitutes. The air in the Constabulary had changed dramatically, chief officers were seen walking about the station a lot more and there were many more closed-door meetings amongst them. Officers' rest days were being cancelled and overtime was being thrown at people. The atmosphere of the towns' public changed also, they seemed much more supportive and often wished us well, it was a nice change but a shame it started because of this.

There was a huge effort being made in trying to reassure the public, and to prevent anything further from happening. The police gave out free attack alarms to women, nightclubs and bars paid for taxis for women to get home safely from their bar or club and the public was now calling in absolutely anything that they thought might help. I remember having to search a field for a sounding alarm, it took me ages but I finally found it and it was a shop bought shed alarm laying in the grass that was going off.

Less than a week after the latest ladies had been reported missing, a second body had been discovered, also in a brook, but this time on the other side of town.

National and International journalists descended on our Constabulary Headquarters, setting up camp on the front lawn. Officers from other Forces had been drafted in, in an attempt at bolstering numbers to allow everyday policing to continue whilst increasing the number of officers dedicated to the hunt for the ladies, there was Police everywhere, and every single one of them was busy.

Obviously, I was now only just into my second patrol year so I was not privy to any of the ongoing investigations other than when I was tasked with something, but even then I was only given the information I needed to know.

Another night and another stint of scene preservation with a colleague, this time on the inner cordon nearer to the first victim. A long slow night shift, trying to stay warm and awake, just in case the media tried to get in. There were a few that would be hell-bent on trying to get a photo or a chat with someone at the scene, not realising they are actually making things harder for the Police recovery and slowing the whole process down.

I had started to gain my own personal dislike of journalists, I understand they have a job to do, but surely in serious circumstances like this, they could contain themselves just a bit! After all, the Constabularies chief officers gave regular press releases and people wouldn't be given any further information unless needed.

One good thing was the aviation laws, the Medias helicopters were not permitted to fly as low as the military or Police so they never got to bother the scenes, the police helicopter controlled the skies around the scenes, so take that!

A couple of days later, a 3rd body was then reported as being found, this time in some undergrowth, but again, just outside the town and another couple of miles from the previous two.

"This was crazy! What the hell is going on!?"
Suffolk on average only had a few murders a year, now we've got 3 bodies in such a short space of time. I had now been an officer for just over a year and a half and I didn't expect this type of thing at all in Suffolk.

The very next day a 5th lady, who was also a prostitute was reported missing.

The day after the latest missing report, I remember I was about to finish a long tiring shift and was going to put my stuff away in my locker, it was then broadcast that a 4th body had now been found. I walked up the stairs and went to the door to speak with my team about it, then only a couple of minutes later the Police helicopter broadcast that they have found a 5th body dumped close by to the 4th. This was utterly insane, I honestly thought this wouldn't stop. *"Who on earth is doing this to people?"* I obviously didn't get to go home!!

These latest 2 bodies had been dumped on the verge of a relatively busy road, just a few hundred yards apart and very close to the road itself. Something that I still continue to find odd is that both bodies had been presumably dumped at the same time but why move 2-300 yards between them?

A week later, I began another shift and was posted at a mobile police station in the red light area, engaging with members of the public and recording down anything that may help the investigation.

During my time there, this really strange and odd guy came up to me really flustered, asking me if he can come inside and write things down about the "girls," he kept asking me questions and saying he knew all of the prostitutes and that their DNA would be all over his car. I left him talking to a colleague and took the opportunity to slip outside to his car which was parked a few metres away, looking inside it was relatively clean and orderly, apart from a single lipstick that was stuffed down between the rear seats. I then noticed that two journalists had seen me and were now approaching me. I quickly stopped what I was doing and went back into the mobile station. The man was still there, head in his hands and very upset.

I compiled a report on this man's interaction with us and then shortly after my relief arrived to take over, so after that, I was off home.

A few hours later, I received a call from a detective, I was needed back at work to write an official statement on my interactions with that man, I was told he was going to be arrested! Wow! My rookie mind thinking, *"Have I found the murderer?"* Following his arrest and interrogation, the answer would be a resounding no.

It would now not be long until the suspected murderer Steve Wright, would be found, arrested, charged and remanded in custody until his trial at the Ipswich Crown Court on January 14th 2008.

Through the hard work and dedication of those investigating the incidents and the public for the really helpful information being provided, he was found guilty at court and on February 21st 2008 he was sentenced to a whole life term in prison.

That was just a very quick snippet of the goings on from my inexperienced eyes as a new patrol officer. There are a number of really good books that go into a lot of detail about the serial killings and I highly recommend you have a read of one if this is a subject you find interesting.

This incident and the feelings I got as a new officer stuck with me and will do forever, I experienced Policing during the time of a Serial Killer! Not something anybody wants to happen, but an experience nonetheless that did happen. It left such a hold on me that during the rest of my career, not a year passed without me visiting the sites where the bodies had been found and paying my respects to them. It was truly a dreadful incident and each one of those ladies, regardless of their need for drugs or prostitution all deserved a longer and happier life than they had.

The next 3 years working in the town saw me grow greatly in confidence and experience. When I first started my career, an area I'd never considered changing was my character, I became increasingly cynical and trusted very few people, I also started to see the world differently too.

What was once a residential street, a handy shopping area, a car park good for a certain restaurant, a picturesque field or country lane were all fast becoming the places I had found a body, an area full of drug addicts and paraphernalia, the place I found a child crying in desperation over their lost parents or the scene of a collision. The world was now changing for me and I had not anticipated that. I was regularly seeing people at their worst and also seeing the worst in people, always suspicious of another's motives and always questioning that which I didn't see.

Day to day Policing is not how it is pictured in the movies or the TV shows, it is often mundane, boring and no matter what you did there was paperwork or computer systems to update, and whenever the government said they had reduced paperwork for the Police, it was true, they had! Except now it was all electronic, still there and still needing to be done. You dealt with the same victims of crime and the same offenders, for the same offences and at the same locations, a never-ending cycle of shit!

It was usually, criminal families calling the Police on other criminal families. It was not very common for a call to come in that had a genuinely innocent victim. For the average law abiding citizen, it is something quite major for them to pick up the phone and call the Police. Instead, it what was the usual; they assaulted me because I broke their fence, because they stole my drugs, because they keyed my car and because they slept with my dog! Circle of events that some people had going on.

The truly innocent victims of crime were the ones I wanted to help, those who had played no part in becoming a victim, and one day shift, I would have that very chance.

I got a call to attend an address following a domestic-related assault, in which a 7-year-old girl had been kicked to the head. When I arrived there was the young 7-year-old girl with her mother, they were both hysterical and the girl was clearly in a bad way following an attack. She had cuts to her arms and face, a swollen lip, grazing to her chin, a badly swollen eye and a really clear, severely inflamed shoe tread pattern on the side of her face.

I discovered that the 7-year-old had been upstairs in her room, and being a typical youngster her room was not that tidy, with toys on the floor and the bed not been made. Her stepfather had apparently asked her to tidy the room up and she had not done so, this had turned him (although he probably always was) psycho.

He hurled her down the first-floor flight of stairs, tumbling all the way to the bottom to the ground floor, and as a result, suffered many of the injuries. But this was not enough for him, with the girl now laying at the base of the stairs injured and very vulnerable, he followed down behind her and then raised his foot and stamped on the side of her face, causing her head to press down hard into the ground. Realising he was now in a world of major league shit, he left the address.

Hearing this account had caused to feel great anger inside me, I was livid. This low-life piece of scum did this to a child and then instead of helping, he flees to protect himself.

With an ambulance now at the scene, I and a colleague concentrated on finding this man, it was not hard! As well as being a low-life he was also bloody stupid, a common trait amongst the criminals I met! After his escape, he had sent a text message to the mother saying he was next door and would come back when things had "calmed down."

My colleague and I requested a further Police unit to attend to assist in the arrest of this man and with us all pumped up over the incident, a quick knock on the door very quickly turned into the door being smashed off its frame. The man was there, and looked very sheepish, unfortunately for us though, he did not resist in the slightest, damn! He would have got bent into all kinds of shapes if he'd tried anything!

He was then arrested for causing Grievous Bodily Harm and taken to Police custody. This case was then handed to the Child protection officers to deal with the man and ensure safeguards were in place for his release.

Whilst in this instance a child was the victim, it was actually, also fairly common for children to be the perpetrator of crime. Sometimes though, the public couldn't believe a child would get into trouble with the Police and could not understand that Police also had to use force against them, in my first few years three of note stood out;

I was on nights double crewed with a colleague and we were asked to attend a small office building where an alarm was going off.

When we arrived, we found a girl aged about 13. She was standing by a ground floor smashed window and nobody else was about. My colleague told her to stand still, but she chose to run, my colleague caught hold of her and whilst holding her arm he started to ask what she had been doing by an office building when it was closed at night, and why the alarm was going off with her found by a smashed ground floor window.

She was a vile child, shouting and cursing at us both and using many expletives. She was told to be more respectful which didn't go down well! With that, she threw a punch towards my colleagues face. Seeing her fist going towards his head I grabbed her by the scruff of the neck and planted her hard, face down into the gravel car park.

A check on her name found her to have a rap sheet of commercial burglaries against her already, but you probably guessed that!

Whilst on a day shift I was walking away from an address following a general workload enquiry. I heard the sound of smashing glass just around the corner from me, as I rounded the corner I saw a ground floor window had been smashed, and an 11-year-old boy was inside putting stuff into a backpack. I shouted at him to get here, he came over but would not come back out of the window, he reckoned he lived there. A check on his name found he had already been dealt with for residential burglaries, and his address was not this one. As he refused to come out the window, I went in and grabbed the feral kid and took him outside, he was squirming about and constantly swearing at me at the top of his voice. Members of the public who would not have seen the build-up to me walking with him, all started to watch, many of them now shouting at me for having hold of a young child and I kept being told to leave him alone. This little shit had made me so angry inside now! I bet the members of the public would have had a different view if he had broken into their house and then behaved like this to them.

The last of these incidents being during a late shift, I was driving along a well-known street, populated mainly by criminals and drug addicts, the kind of street you see car parts, mattresses, washing machines and general waste in people's front gardens.

This 12-year-old girl decided it would be funny to keep running out in front of me, causing me to brake to a stop, she'd move, I'd go and she'd do it again. I then gave her a damn good ear deafening siren note to move her away, she then decided that warranted kicking the front of my car, a number of times.

Many of the local yobs were now gathering in the street, watching this debacle unfold. I got out and gave her a damn good mouthful, the kind her parents should have done many years ago. She then thought it was a good idea to kick me with all her might on my shin, the little brat!

I went to grab her and she went to run off, I stuck my foot out and she fell, rolling to a stop. I then went to arrest her, and take her to our custody, and then she started flailing her legs around repeatedly kicking at my legs. I had to pin her hard into the ground just to cuff the little brat. With that, all of the resident yobs started shouting at me, I was apparently a child abuser, a paedophile and a bully. And people wonder why I started to hate the public! Even as I write this I feel contempt for parts of society taking over me!

As my views at work were changing, so too, was it affecting my mind at home. Nothing too serious but my work was certainly making things more interesting, but not for my partner! Dealing with such an array of incidents in a high-stress environment led to frequent and strong dreams about things I'd dealt with.

A summer's late shift and I was single crewed covering a new larger area of the town. There was a call for an ongoing assault in an alleyway behind a convenience store. I was right there, just a few seconds away! As I turned up, I could see in the dim light two men close together and a lot of moving around of the limbs, although at this point I didn't know what exactly was occurring. As they became aware of my presence, they stopped, one of the men looked towards me then ran off in the opposite direction. I approached the remaining male who was shouting out in what I initially thought was pain, but turned out to be more of a mad panic. I then saw a hypodermic needle sticking out of his neck, the man was in a real stress and pulled it out and threw it on the floor.

In amongst the shouting and fretting I found out he had been inside the store and when he came out he was grabbed by the attacker who had now run away.

The attacker had threatened to stab him unless he handed over any money and a phone, but the man put up a fight and the attacker then stabbed the hypodermic needle into his neck and tried hitting him, that's when I appeared on the scene and you know the rest…

That night at home and asleep in my bed I started having a dream, one I can still remember vividly. I was at work and inside someone's house dealing with an angry man, the man then went to stab me with a hypodermic needle. This had caused me to slightly stir, conscious but still asleep I tried to fend the attacker off by swinging a metal teapot for his face, striking him to the nose. What had actually happened mind you, was slightly different! I was awoken fully by a cry of shock from my partner who was now holding her nose, I immediately realised I had struck out issuing a palm strike at her in my sleep! It took a tad of apologising from me for that one!

Whilst these things that police deal with are not very nice, you occasionally, and very rarely to be honest with you, get to see some sheer delights.

My colleague and I responded to a report of damage caused inside a town centre bar. When we arrived, the bar was still full of revellers and we were shown some smashed glass screens, the manager knew the offender and also told us where she lived. We turned up at an apartment in a block of flats nearby and started to bang on the door, soon a female voice was heard to tell us to go away. So she's inside we now knew, so the door was swiftly smashed in and inside we went.

We were greeted by a stunning 20 something-year-old lady with neatly brushed shoulder length straight brown hair, and wearing a long light blue dressing gown, she wasn't rude or offensive to us but clearly didn't want us there. She was also drunk & very upset. We told her why we were there and that she was to be placed under arrest for the criminal damage.

This set off a bucket full of tears and worry about her job, we told her to get herself decent and then she had to come with us.

She went into the bathroom, leaving the door ajar, at our request (to ensure she does not lock it and self-harm or arm herself with anything to then harm us with). We stood at the door checking on her but also trying to give her a little privacy, she then started to shout and moan in disbelief, as she shouted something like, *"I can't take this!"* we flung the door open expecting her about to self-harm, but in fact she threw open her dressing gown and dropped to her knees facing us, completely naked! After a brief second to catch our breath – she was extremely gifted with good looks and very pleasant to the eye – we got her tied up in her dressing gown, grabbed some random clothes and took her to the Police cells.

On a warm summer's night shift, a few years down the line… A colleague and I were patrolling one of the main dual carriageways in the county, when we saw a taxi pull up abruptly in front of us, leaving it now stationary in a dangerous position, we pulled up behind it and had our rear lights on, known as a fend off, providing some safety.

Just before we got out to investigate, two young ladies wearing mini-skirts and tank tops got out of the taxi and whilst facing away from us bent right over and proceeded to throw up their night's drinks! With the view we were now presented with, but also with the act being performed by them, it was a difficult decision on whether it pleasing to the eye or not!

Even in a moment of life's collapse, it seemed some people could still have an air of beauty about them, others, on the other hand, you remember for all the wrong reasons;

A late shift with a different colleague, we were called to attend an address to remove a drunk lady who was refusing to leave. We arrived in a heavily populated street and once at the address, we found a prosthetic leg laying on the front lawn by the door, ok…

We got invited inside by the homeowner and were led down a corridor, passing a huge pool of human wee on the floor as we went into the living room, there we were greeted by another prosthetic leg laying on the floor and a very large lady laying on her back with her two residual limbs facing towards us, she too was completely naked.

Once we had remembered we weren't in a gynaecology unit, we told this lady to get dressed, put her clothes on, put her legs on and get out! She was very abusive, shouting, swearing and then she proceeded to urinate all over the couch like a lawn sprinkler system, classy bitch! She refused to leave which left us no choice, she was to be arrested.

Unfortunately, between ourselves and the owner, we now had to force clothes on to her and then had to carry her out by her arms, she was placed into a Police van along with her legs and taken away.

One last example of a classy person was on yet another night shift. A colleague and I were patrolling an estate, we saw a vehicle with a light out and decided to follow it and see where it was going. Within a minute or so, it pulled up at an address and a scantily clad lady got out, seeing our car now stationary a bit further back she walked up to us, she was wearing a really short skirt and basically just a bra on the top half. As she came up to the car she was yelling at us in an indecipherable drunken language, I wound down my window and when she got to the door she said *"I bet you want some of this!"* and with that flung her right foot up onto the window ledge and spread her legs, revealing to us that she had obviously forgotten to put any underwear on, *"No you're alright thanks very much"* I remarked, and off she went shouting some drawl as she went.

As you are seeing, Police officers are constantly being exposed to things that most private citizens don't get to see or even hear about, the Police have to deal with a lot of repeated trauma and a lot of mental strain, leaving images being stored up in their minds that stay there forever, smells that cling to your memory like they are stuck in your nose and sounds of pain associated with another's suffering emanating in their ears for eternity. By reading on you will see more of what I am explaining, could you just forget?

Due to all the units being used up, I had to attend a property in a neighbouring area after it was reported that a young man had just been injured, the ambulance service was also en route but had not yet arrived. As I drew up a few people were jumping around flagging me down in the street, all in a mad and desperate panic.

I stopped and got out, they were shouting for me to hurry up and they rushed me round to the back of the house where I could clearly see a garden party had been going on.

In the middle of the garden was a huge bonfire burning away, with plastic chairs around it in a ring, many of which had toppled over and some were melting in the fire. Beer bottles were all over the place, and tables of food were laid against the fences around the edge of the property.

I got led over towards the back door where a man was laying on the ground, screaming in utter agony, a really high pitched and ear-bursting scream! His clothes had practically all but melted away, leaving patches of cloth stuck to his now severely red and blistering body, his face almost unrecognisable and his head, bald with tight red skin.

Everyone was in a panic, they had all been drinking and thought it wise to run around, and over the fire, using the chairs as stepping stones, this man had unfortunately fallen in, become entangled in the large amounts of burning wood and melting plastic of the chairs, before he was pulled fully ablaze from the fire and dragged away by his drunken friends, sadly not very quickly. There was nothing I could do, not a single thing, he died right there before me.

As I am repeatedly saying, because for the Police it is repeatedly, they put themselves in harm's way to instil peace and order so others can go about their lives with minimal disturbance.

Assaults on Police Officers are unfortunately inevitable, they have to take away peoples liberties, and often at a time, the person doesn't want it taken away But, it shouldn't have to happen at all.

During my first few years I had already been assaulted a number of times whilst doing my duty, but what happens next was the first time I saw the courts award me any form of compensation for my injuries, sustained helping others;

In the spring of 2007, I and another officer attended one of the local high schools, this was following a report of an excluded student being at the gate with a baseball bat shouting and swearing at people within the school grounds.

When we arrived, nobody was there, so we spoke with the head of school and we were told that a 15-year-old boy had recently been excluded for assaulting staff, and for the last couple of days he has appeared at the school brandishing the baseball bat and threatening to hit the staff when they leave at the end of the day, so far the incident had not progressed beyond that.

With school soon finishing we went for a short drive to return just before kicking out time.

When we returned, low and behold there was a lad with a bat shouting at the gate. We approached him and told him to move away from the gates, he started to shout and swear at us and luckily by us slowly moving backwards from him, he followed, still shouting at us. This was helpfully leading him away from the gate where other children would soon be exiting from.

We spoke to him about the problem he was causing and the offence he was committing, which started to calm him down a bit. My colleague then went to arrest him and the lad not liking that, swung his bat with full might, striking my right hand across the knuckles, it hurt! And that annoyed me! I discharged a can of spray right in his face and he dropped like a baby squirming and screaming on the floor, I then dropped my body to make my knee come down full force on to the back of the hand holding the bat, he was in tatters! He was restrained without much further effort, handcuffed and then taken to the cells.

Shortly afterwards, my hand had started to swell up so I had to attend the local hospital for an X-ray, where I was told I had suffered a hairline fracture by one of the knuckle joints and had to spend a while with finger restraints on to aid it's healing.

A case file was later prepared and the brat appeared at court, he was found guilty of possessing an offensive weapon and assault on Police. He was then ordered to pay £50 / $80-90 to me by way of compensation.

I came to realise that when Policing, there were two types of private citizen, the type that loves the Police and help them whenever they can and the type that would complain at everything and also attack them.

Sometimes somebody being "helpful" would actually hinder us and then there were times it was amusing seeing someone play "cop" for a moment, this was one those incidents I had come across;

I had been sent to a residential street where the owners of a home had returned following a long vacation, and wanted to report that their house had been broken into and their basement was flooded due to some stolen water pipes.

The baddies had broken into the basement of the home and stolen a large amount of copper piping, this copper piping was for the water in the house, and at the time demanded a high value as scrap metal, and its theft had subsequently flooded the basement.

To make matters worse, the property formed part of a block of terraced houses which were on a steep hill, so the flooding had led downhill to neighbouring properties causing those to also become flooded.

I knocked on doors and confirmed flooding down the hill house by house as I went. I got to one and there was no answer, I was banging on the door and shouting through the doors mailbox, for a good 10 minutes.

Due to the proven damage to a number of properties above this one, it was highly likely water had flooded into this one's basement causing extensive damage too. I would have to force entry to check for and prevent damage, and if confirmed, alert the appropriate authorities for pumping the water away.

A man who had been walking down the street had seen me paying a lot of attention in this house and asked if he could help with anything. He was tall and really overweight! Yes, I thought, he could barge the back door down for me.

I told him of my plan and he was very excited, for him it was probably a once in a lifetime opportunity to knock a door down without any come back on him. I should add that these houses were all old Victorian-era homes, and this particular one had a very old wooden back door.

He conjured up as much energy as possible, and decided to run at it, he looked like a rutting rhino trying to get to his favourite mate. It killed me inside, he clearly watches too many action movies! He ran into the door with all of his of might and the whole bloody thing, door, frame, lock, hinges, everything, fell inwards in a cloud of dust and debris, leaving a brick edged hole where the door and frame once stood, well that worked! Almost instantly a woman was then heard screaming and shouting, the man for some reason, now terrified, ran behind me, *"guess what chap? You can't hide when you're that big!"* I thought.

We were quickly met by a middle-aged woman holding a cast iron fire poker who thought she was being burgled and upon seeing me she stopped in her tracks, in utter shock. I told her what was, and had occurred, and she claimed she didn't hear me knocking! Well, as it turned out her basement was flooded too, and the electrical fuse box was in the basement. Good job I wasn't afraid of using the powers given to the Police.

As time went on working in the town, I knew this was not the kind of Policing I wanted to do, I had slowly become very annoyed and disheartened with the kind of work being presented to me and was faced with a decision.

I needed to get away from the massive and never-ending workloads of the re-active Policing I was part of. I wanted to join the Roads Policing Unit and deal with serious collisions, chase baddies and be pro-active! I was getting very little chance to be pro-active in town and build any evidence of my experience for Roads Policing, which wasn't helping my mood.

The final straw came when I was asked to attend a neighbourly dispute…

It was a quiet estate with houses and property lines divided by low 2ft high brick walls. When I arrived I had literally only just stopped the car, and as is very common in policing, a man came running over to me shouting and gesticulating before I'd even opened the door! I got out and told him to calm down and speak clearly to me, he was really livid about something.

He told me to follow him and he'd show me what this was all about, we walked up his driveway towards his house and he led me to the dividing wall and whilst pointing to a flower pot with black duct tape covering parts of it he said, *"Look at that, how can he put that there? It is not at all aesthetically pleasing!"* Really!!! Is that it??? For fuck sake! I told the man in no uncertain terms to grow up and get on with it, calling the Police on 999 over how a plant pot – which he didn't even own – was repaired and looked was pathetic.

I walked off, got in my car and went to see the Inspector for my shift. I had had it, I didn't want this anymore. I told him my thoughts of Policing in the town and that I was seriously considering leaving the Force if this is all policing had to offer me.

He tried reassuring me with the usual corporate ball-shit, *"you're doing a great job, you are well respected etc. etc....."* I left it with, *"I would like a move to a rural station so I can gain some proactive experience or I will be resigning."*

Well... A few days later he came to me and said there is a place at Hadleigh Town. It was a little town, with a population of about 8,000 residents and a rural patrol area totalling about 44,000 residents, if I'd like it. Yep, Thankyou I would. This was great!

I started working at my new station in 2009. Working the Hadleigh area was a completely different beast to Ipswich, there would be 2 or 3 emergency jobs a day and sometimes none! It was honestly as though nothing happened! It would make a great place for officers to see out their last few years before retirement.

The positive side to this was any crimes that did occur, I think got a much more thorough investigation and you had more time to be with the victims trying to help and reassure them, you could conduct house 2 house enquiries and prepare any evidential paperwork to a much greater standard without the fear being pulled away for yet another job. The number of times, I'd previously just arrived at someone's house to take a statement, or driven miles to make an enquiry and as soon I started I was dispatched to another emergency incident I cannot quantify, it was a very regular occurrence.

I could now deal with crime properly and be pro-active, actually go and target traffic offences, check up on disqualified drivers, hunt for drink drivers, spend time talking to and explaining why people were being antisocial when racing their cars about in a car park in the dead of night, and compared to the last 4 years where I would always be asked to attend another job whilst still dealing with one, this was bliss! This was what I thought it would be like when I joined.

I had only worked there a few weeks before my enthusiasm and drive was noticed and led to me being temporarily (8-9 months) promoted to being the Sergeant for the shift, this was whilst the substantive Sergeant was posted to another area. This gave me even more opportunity to build evidence for any future Roads Policing application.

Sadly, working in Hadleigh wasn't always good news…

One day shift, there was a call to attend a nearby river, this was due to a report of an 8-year-old child having fallen in and become unconscious from drowning.

After only a few minutes' drive I had arrived, and whilst searching for the caller, I found there was a grassy walkway along a river bank, with a group of Adults who were crowded around the lifeless body of a young child.

It transpired they and some other children were out for a planned hike, the child had somehow fallen into the river and being unable to swim, the child quickly drowned.

When the child had been pulled from the water an attempt at saving the child's life had begun. I quickly took over CPR, chest compressions on the child, desperate to bring them back. Sweat was dripping from my head and my hands and arms were cramping up, this was the hardest thing I had done. With the mixture of adrenaline, fear, and determination, this was easily the most tiring thing imaginable. Luckily another colleague arrived and took over, and continued in the effort of saving the kids life.

I was then informed that one of the adults had called the child's parents, who had now arrived. Whilst screaming hysterically and shouting for their child, I had to keep them away, it was the best thing whilst lifesaving treatment was ongoing. They must have thought I was a horrible and uncaring person, I was in fact, the very opposite. They would not have been able to perform CPR on their own dying child as well as somebody unrelated and also trained and experienced, plus they would have got in the way of the efforts being made. They also didn't, in my opinion, need the image of their child's chest being repeatedly compressed down stored in their memory forever.

Despite everyone's best efforts, the child was unfortunately pronounced dead at the scene by a later attending paramedic.

This was the 1st time I had done CPR on anyone other than the rubber training dummy "Annie" once a year. In reality it was hard work, bloody shattering, and not like the movies, any thought of, this many compressions and then this many breaths went far from my mind, you become fixated on just doing something to save the person, not an act I would want to repeat but unfortunately, this later became quite a regular part of my working life that would see me perform CPR on at least 50 separate people, sometimes with a good result but more often than not the injuries proved too devastating to support life.

The image of the lifeless child and the feeling of the chest being pressed down remains very fresh in my mind to this day. I couldn't have done any more for that little one.

Whilst at Hadleigh, the Force underwent a slight change of uniform, gone were the hideous woolly jumpers and they were replaced with a fleece zip-up top, these were much comfier.

Also, a slight appointments change, out with the CS spray and in came something called PAVA. This was much more potent and had the benefits of only affecting the person it hits, unlike CS that got everyone in the resulting cloud. The downside to this was you had to be more accurate, it would only work if it got into someone's eye. Aim for the face and forehead, it just needed a drop, and from experience, I can tell you it hurt! Clamping your eyes shut and unable to see, it was a good new piece of kit.

My posting to Hadleigh provided me with the next driving course, albeit a shorter one... The 4x4 course.

Some time spent alone with the instructor driving through muddy fields and down tiny farm tracks, then some high-speed work. This was completed in a Ford Ranger pickup truck with a hard top bed cover. It was an alright motor and reasonably fun to take off road but, I preferred the handling of cars much more. Another successfully completed driving course and another patch on my arm.

A few months into my stint at Hadleigh there was an opening at the Headquarters Roads Policing Unit, with applications being accepted from anyone who had successfully completed their first 2 years. This is what I had been waiting for, this is what I had been working towards and this was what I wanted, so badly!

The application paper was a typical Police application with questions based on only a few subjects;
Tell me a time you had to deal with Race and Diversity?
Tell me a time you showed Personal Responsibility?
Tell me a time you worked as a Team? And so on. There was only a small section for why you wanted to join and whether you feel you could pass the Police Advanced Driving Course.

There wasn't a very big timeframe before the applications closed so I had to get on with it. I filled it out with all of my newly collated evidence of good work and leadership and sent it in, hoping for the best.

If day shifts were quiet at Hadleigh you can only imagine how quiet the night shift was, starting at 11 pm I would conduct the briefing of my team of 3 officers, covering anything which had occurred of significance and give out patrol routes, on nights we double-crewed and I went out with one of the officers to patrol.

We would check the industrial estates, areas of previous burglaries, stop and check the documents of many cars, and help adjoining areas if they were busier than us. We would go back in at about 3 am for our ref's break and if not deployed, watch the 1st half of a movie (the second half would be the next night shift), then back out for a quick check of the roads and nearby farms before finishing time was upon us.

In the Police there is a department named CID, the Criminal Investigation Department, they are people who have done an advanced investigative course and should have, and they even say they should have, responsibility for investigating major crime and residential burglaries, unless it seemed, there was a crime they were already investigating, and therefore couldn't possibly have more than 1 to do at a time.

Patrol officers had to investigate as many crimes as they took reports for, but not them! I dare say there were some that would actually do more work and have good workloads, instead of seeing it as a way of escaping patrol work, but from my experience, that was not the norm amongst the CID officers that I met.

Every rape, murder, burglary that they were called for, the response was nearly always *"Can uniform (frontline officers) attend"* The officers would then do all the initial "golden hour" (quick time priority investigations to find and capture the most valuable evidence) tasks, and once things were calm or even the next day then CID would take ownership of it, if they could!

In late 2009, there was a spate of residential burglaries in the quiet town of Hadleigh. I went and took the numerous reports and although I knew the answer, I asked if any CID officer would take on the investigation, guess what? They couldn't deal with them due to "other enquiries," never mind I knew they wouldn't anyway.

Following on from the enquiries of scenes of crime officers putting pixie dust everywhere to show up any fingerprints, house to house visits to gain any witness information possible and trawling the different areas for CCTV cameras, I came up with the names of 3 possible reprobates and got together a small team of officers to go and get them.

A couple of days later and at stupid o'clock in the morning, usually 3-5am, the teams were split to attend each person's address and "wake them up."

Being trained to use what is known as the "big red key" (a very heavy single person battering ram, coloured red!) I smashed one of the front doors in and in we all went making as much noise as possible (shock and awe), finding the person needed and cuffing them. We then set about a search of the property and low and behold found some of the property stolen from the burglaries.

With 3 people arrested, paperwork completed and evidence recovered they were dealt with by the courts. Their sentence was 36 weeks night-time curfew! That's it!! Still, I did my job and got something out of it at the end.

It was not long before I got told I had passed the paper application for Roads Policing and had been invited to attend an interview with the Roads Policing senior command.

The interview took place about 2 weeks later and I was asked the same questions as the paper application, and then they asked me about some experiences I'd had and any evidence I had gathered to join the Dept. I felt the interview was going well, I had plenty to say and thanks to being at Hadleigh, I had some good evidence of self-initiated work I'd done. I left there feeling positive and was told I'd hear within a week.

December 2009, in my personal life, my now wife was heavily pregnant and due any day with our first child, life was going really well, and I was feeling very positive. This reflected in my work also, I had so much drive and passion, I was calling up for almost every job I could, dealing with offences and getting some good results. I was on a cloud it felt.

The day we brought my first born child, a girl, back home from the hospital I had a phone call from a Roads

Policing senior officer, I was told my application was successful and my start date was at the beginning of February 2010.

How over the moon was I!!!? I was now joining the Roads Policing Unit. I had looked up to these people my whole career and watched in awe whenever they drove past in the much nicer cars! And looked on in envy whenever they took over from me at serious collisions.

The Roads Policing Units main roles at the time were; reducing the number of fatal and serious injury collisions, denying criminals the use of the road, preventing antisocial use of motor vehicles and countering terrorism. The Dept. would if needed, assist local patrols in incidents if there was a shortage of patrol staff or a danger to officers and or the public. They would not, however, be used as a first response by the control room for incidents that should be dealt with by the local patrols. This kept us free to Police the big roads and be available for serious collisions and incidents.

The Department at that time, was made up of just over 40 officers stationed at 3 bases covering the entire county's road network, totalling just over 4038 miles of maintained road. There was a base at the Police Headquarters (the number one garage!), a base at Bury St Edmunds (the number two garage, also known compassionately as BK's, 'Bury Knobbers') and a base at Halesworth.

Due to the nature of the incidents we attended and the associated risks posed to the public, we were mainly dealing with Grade A incidents. It was extremely rare for a Roads Policing car to be dispatched to an incident that did not require an immediate emergency response. When considering the size of the Roads Policing Unit and the fact they dealt with the greatest majority of grade 'A' incidents that came through to the Constabulary, you can see it was a very fast paced environment.

To help with a little understanding for any readers in the USA or those that don't know the area, I am going to help out a bit. - This will come in handy as you read about my time within the Roads Policing Unit.

UK	U.S. EQUIVALENT
70mph Multi-Lane Carriageway/Road. Also Dual Carriageway or Motorway	Interstate, more than one lane for each direction of traffic
Vehicle Bonnet	Hood
Vehicle Boot	Trunk
Windscreen	Windshield
Exhaust	Muffler
Drive on the left	Drive on the right
Tyres	Tires
Articulated Goods Vehicle Artic lorry	40 ton, 18 wheel tractor-trailer
Registration Plate	Vehicle tag

Suffolk is a rural county with a few 70mph multi-lane roads in it. The A14, this road went from East to West through the county and was the busiest main road in the county which had over 80,000 vehicles us it daily. The A12, this road went from south to north through the county joining with London and this had over 57,000 vehicles use it daily. There were also some main arterial routes that were extremely busy and gave us a lot of work, the main one being the A140, this was a single carriageway – 1 lane in each direction, this road also went south to north through the county and had over 26,000 vehicles use it daily. That'll be enough to help. It's a lot of vehicles!

Before my start date, I made some visits to the Roads Policing Unit to get my kit ready, check where lockers and things are kept, to have their private radio talk group added to my radio and I also met the officer who was going to tutor me for the first 10 weeks of my time on the unit.

Tutoring was very much needed as I would now be policing the big roads with high speeds, getting involved in and having greater responsibility for the much more serious incidents. Generally working in a much more dangerous environment.

I take life at my own pace, I walk slow – annoying to most people with me, I am quiet, I don't get very easily flustered and I like to take my time over things. The officer who was going to be tutoring me was the complete opposite! I didn't know what to expect, he was LOUD!! Walked fast, ate fast, made cups of tea fast, everything he did was as though it was his last ever chance to do it and I was genuinely worried there was going to be a serious clash of personalities.

It would turn out very different and to this day I still consider him a very good friend and I thank him from the bottom of my heart for helping me get settled and for turning me into someone who was greatly respected and liked within the unit.

© Jeremy H Cohen. My first RP team, taken autumn 2010. I'm 2nd from the left, my tutor is far right.

I turned up for day one at the HQ Roads Policing Unit with a shiny and clean new Hi-Vis jacket and a brand new kit bag for my paperwork, I met my new team and got acquainted with the new building and different places kit was kept.

I was shown all of the equipment in the cars; this was very different from the standard patrol car, now I'd have In-built speed detection equipment, Automatic Number Plate Recognition (ANPR) systems, stolen vehicle trackers, cameras and speakers and a whole host of road safety equipment in the back, 12 cones, 6 self-standing signs, 3 Armco barrier signs, blue flashing lamps, spade, shovel, crowbar, broom, padlocks and cables (for locking vehicles up), a Stinger (a spiked tyre deflation system for pursuits), reams of paperwork for Serious and Fatal collisions, the list goes on, basically everything needed to shut a major road and deal with major incidents. This was very different from my old standard patrol car which had a couple of cones, 1 or 2 bent up signs and a Snickers wrapper stuffed in the door pocket!

Over the next couple of days, we went out and I was shown some of the best locations used for speed detection and traffic monitoring, how to get into the Port, which was Britain's premier boat port and got to see how some of the equipment worked. From here on we would then patrol and respond (him driving, I still needed my Advanced course for these cars) to incidents.

I also had a new list of required evidence to pass this new tutor period, things like, deal with speed and phone offences, deal with a collision on a major road, close a major road, deal with offences involving commercial goods vehicles and be the OIC (Officer in Charge) for fatal collisions...... with the speed of my colleague and the amount of incidents that occurred we did this fairly easily.

I still remember the first blue light run with me in a Roads Policing Car as an RP Officer, our allocated car was a Police Spec Ford Mondeo ST220, a 3.0 V6, which went 0-62mph in 6.6 seconds and had a top speed of 155mph[5], it was a lowered, sportier version of the family-friendly version and whilst it was slower at accelerating compared to what I would get in the future, it was a bloody awesome car. It held the road like a Go-Kart and went much quicker than my previous patrol car. With its rapid pace and awesome cornering ability, it was a tough car to beat.

We attended an incident and when the Blue lights and Siren went on, and the engine sang in the high rev range the feeling of self-pride and achievement made me well up inside, a feeling of utter appreciation for the car and me now in a department that I had looked at in awe, I could feel myself get a tear in my eye with the pride I now felt.

Although I would never lose the absolute buzz of driving these machines at high speeds and on the limit through series' of bends, they would, however, become just another tool of my trade. A feeling that will stay with me forever was that of two RP cars going along the dual carriageway both at 130+ mph in procession was awesome, and when two were in procession at speed on the twisty country roads, it was a joy to behold and something I will be sad to have lost.

It didn't take long for me to understand that feeling of having to get, and have, control of major incidents like my tutor had often spoken of.

In the spring of 2010, during the early hours of the morning, we were dispatched to attend a collision, one that would turn out to be my first fatal collision as an RP Officer.

It had occurred on a stretch of wide and fast country road about 50 minutes from our base.

As we had to attend from some distance away, by the time we got there the Ambulance service, fire brigade and a couple of local police patrols were already there. It had been confirmed en route that one of the people involved had been pronounced dead. I remember as we arrived my tutor said to me, *"remember you are now a Traffic Cop, we are in control of this incident"* and he also told me to get out and start to fill in a particular form, the fatal collision scene managers notebook.

I got out of the car amongst all the other emergency personnel and put my white topped cap on (only worn by Roads Policing Officers), and immediately upon seeing this

Fire Chiefs and Ambulance commanders wanted to speak with me, I felt so out of my depth but discussed what they had done prior to our arrival, and what was now required of them. My tutor providing a pillar of support throughout was greatly appreciated, after all, he had done this for years.

We walked the scene to get an idea of what was there and who was about, and being in the dark with blue lights flashing against the trees and vehicles, bright lamps lighting the immediate scene and everyone busy, there was a huge feeling of responsibility on me that hadn't existed before, someone had died, and I was responsible for getting things in order.

I saw a sports car with substantial all over damage just off the road in the verge, and a dead body lying on the ground some distance away from it (after being thrown from the car), and there was a very clear debris trail leading back down the road showing the car had been out of control for some time. I started collecting the information that this "fatal collision" paperwork asked of me, and handed out some tasks to the local police. It was odd, with my white hat now on nobody was questioning my decisions and there was a significant change in how respectful people were towards me, I could definitely get used to this!

It was found out that the car had been travelling at high speed and with the driver drunk it soon went out of control, resulting in spinning and rolling which subsequently threw the now deceased person from the vehicle.

Once things had settled down a bit, with witness information taken, occupants of the car identified and the Fire brigade removed from the scene, we set about speaking to the only other occupant of the sports car, it transpired that this person was the driver of the sports car, but not the owner. He had been asked to drive by the owner who was the passenger, and also now dead. A quick summary of what had happened was taken from him and then, as is the case with every collision, a breath test was conducted on the driver, he was well over the drink drive limit.

In the UK the drink drive limits are 35 microgrammes of alcohol per 100 millilitres of breath, 80 milligrammes of alcohol per 100 millilitres of blood and 107 milligrammes of alcohol per 100 millilitres of urine.

Once this had been done he was taken to hospital by the Ambulance, although uninjured it was for a precautionary check over, due to the mechanics of the collision.

I then had to check the dead body for identification, lifting his lifeless cold limbs one by one, checking the pockets for a wallet or any other documents with a name and address on. Once this was discovered, another police unit was dispatched immediately to that address, to speak with any other occupants of the address, and to hopefully identify a next of kin.

With the scene now controlled and the evidence gathering going well, daylight was starting to break and as the darkness lifted it showed in full light the extent of our scene, the distance covered being close to a mile. It also gave me a strange thought; during the night, as people slept quietly in their beds someone had died on the road and we had been in attendance and nobody would have known, as daylight broke these people would be getting up with no change to their lives, except one family who now had to cope with the loss of someone through the actions of a drunk driver.

With any death that the Police attend, a private ambulance is requested on behalf of the coroner of the county to collect the body and remove it to the mortuary for the coroner to examine.

Once they arrived at our scene, we lifted the body onto the stretcher and covered it in a dark red velvet blanket, it was loaded into the ambulance and taken to the mortuary.

Owing to the fact a formal identification had not yet been done, my tutor and I followed closely behind to register it into the mortuary log book, a way of keeping the continuity of the body's identification until a formal ID takes place.

We arrived and once inside we signed the body into the book, and then with the help of the mortuary assistant began the process of undressing the body for the fridge. Which, unless you've done it, is much harder than it seems, a dead weight, cold and stiffening figure is not easy to manipulate. If clothing was not too damaged, we would try our hardest to prevent cutting it off or further damaging it in case it transpired it was the next of kin's favourite outfit, or they wanted it back as a permanent reminder of the persons smell or fondest memories. Once this was all done I slid the body into the fridge alongside the other dead bodies as its company.

Our job here was now done, a long drive back to our base where being late off and completing paperwork for whoever would end up being the investigating officer now laid ahead of us.

So what happens at a fatal collision scene? You may ask. Perhaps you've been diverted due to one or think the Police keep a road closed unnecessarily.

It may surprise you, but it is almost identical to a minor injury collision, with the injury and depth and techniques of the investigation being the main differences.

An assessment is made whether other motorists can move past the scene without disturbing any evidence at the scene, or any signs of the impending collision prior to the scene. We have to think, can the deceased person be identified by passing motorists? Or by the appearance of the vehicle involved? Nobody would want a relative to happen across the fatal crash of a loved one. Will allowing the public near to the scene hinder an investigation? Will allowing other motorists to drive past cause a further collision and risk injury to emergency staff dealing with the collision? For a fatal and life-altering collision, it is almost always a full closure of the road, motorists and/or pedestrians are not allowed near and I wholeheartedly agree with this.

Are any of the public at the scene witnesses? We need their contact details and ideally a statement. Are they involved and trying to pass off as just a witness to it? Once these questions are answered and the necessary details are taken, the scene is cleared of people who are not required any longer, this allows space for a collision reconstruction to occur.

All markings and debris need to be identified, in the grass, on the kerb, on the road, on the vehicle and anywhere else evidence transfer has occurred, every contact leaves a trace. Then, using scanners and advanced imaging equipment a true to life 3D copy of the entire scene is made, allowing computer software to re-create a digital depiction of the scene.

Then, using data such as marks on the road or on the vehicle, an accurate reconstruction of the moments leading up to the collision can be made. This may sound quick but takes a good few hours to get captured correctly and accurately. Once all of this is done, evidence gathering at the scene is completed. We then have to wait on the vehicles being recovered and bodily fluids being professionally cleaned away. Following this, the scene is opened, but there's still lots to do though!!! Which I'll discuss separately in this book.

Have you ever complained that the police have kept a road closed for too long following a fatal collision? Maybe on the face of it, it was a single vehicle collision into a tree, known as a "DODI" (dead one did it), or as an "own goal" collision.

Imagine that this is your loved one involved, police saw this and took less information and closed it off as a DODI, enabling the road to be opened sooner and fewer motorists being inconvenienced. How would you feel if you found out sometime later that your loved one had actually reacted to the presence of another road user, causing them to crash and die? Your loved one, now innocent and killed by another's actions, but with the Police focusing on opening the road quicker, they had failed to spot perhaps the slightest, smallest piece of evidence pointing towards another person or vehicle being involved who was not at the scene. A piece of evidence that could have given them a chance at catching the person and having them sentenced. You'd be pretty pissed off! And probably want blood! I know I would!!!

Fatal and life-altering collisions are bloody serious incidents, the Police must, and in fact have a duty to the people involved, the families, the law and the coroner to conduct a thorough investigation, and work through varying hypotheses' until they can say what the most likely cause of someone being gone FOREVER actually was. I'm sure you would agree it is something that must be done properly!

In May of 2010, I was due to start my 4-week advanced driving course, and man I was looking forward to this! The training cars, both unmarked, were a Ford Mondeo ST220 with a manual gearbox like I'd been in the last few weeks and a Volvo V70 T6, this car was also really nice.

This course was very similar to the 3-week standard response course I had completed except, the speeds were significantly higher, the over-takes were tighter and driving distances were much greater. You were expected to show much more precision with the driving and have a much greater level of observation, anticipation and handling.

Something I had not yet covered about the driving courses was the tea stops! We went to some lovely places and in particular the 'Knicat Bakery' in Downham Market. They had homemade cakes and pastries that were top class, I always had the individual lemon meringue pie and cup of tea. It was sublime!

On one day of the course, we had gone up to the north of the country, to try blatting around some new and unknown areas. On the way back down the A1(M) Motorway, I was driving the ST220, and I loved driving this machine, it took a bend at speeds other cars would slide off the road, it screamed when you floored the throttle, and it wanted to go fast! We were thumping along steady at about 140mph as we rapidly caught up with a patrolling Roads Policing vehicle from this area. I was in lane 4 of the motorway and passed it like a missile, making it disappear into the distance behind me. A few moments later I could then see in the rear mirror the distant image of the patrol car, now with its blue lights lit, it was trying to catch us, obviously unaware of who we were. We continued at a stalemate for a few miles before we backed off and let it identify who we were, it soon dropped away and we continued to make dust. That was such a great feeling!

As any professionally trained driver will admit to, there are days you misjudge the limit point of a bend or miss the odd overtake, and then there are days you are in the zone, nothing can go wrong, it's as though you have a mental, overhead map of the road and can see all the upcoming bends, other cars and hazards ahead, it was as though your plans were all laid out.

I had such a day again in the ST, we were driving a route that to be honest was an awesome driver's road, tight bends, open bends, crests and straights, it had everything. It was the A1066 near Thetford heading towards Ipswich. Even the weather was in our favour, slightly overcast with no glaring sun and a nice dry road surface.

I was hammering along this road, catching everything and within a few bends I was out and passing them, the ST's engine singing, the gears being worked and not a second of backing off to be had, when I finished my drive, I can still remember the instructor saying; *"Thank God!"* apparently his eyes were on stalks trying to keep up with and process what I was doing as we hossed along. He also remarked: *"That was intense!"* What an incredible feeling, I loved that drive and as mentioned I can almost remember it turn by turn to this day. It was like being paid to be a racing car driver but on the open roads, with real hazards and unknown factors thrown in to keep you on your toes.

A fighter pilot once said in his own biography, that driving a Roads Policing vehicle on a fast run was like flying a jet through the mountains. I've never flown a plane but with the amount you have to process in such short spaces of time whilst at high speeds in a performance vehicle, it is incredible.

During the course we spent a while at a military airbase with some cars that had been seized from uninsured motorists and then disclaimed, spinning them around, trying out "J" Turning and racing each other around, evasive driving is great fun! And whilst we were busy training, so to were the military, who seized the opportunity to use our vehicles for close target acquisition practice for the Apache attack helicopters.

The base commander said they don't get to target vehicles driven in this manner when training, so had to take advantage of it. I thought it was brilliant, us training and them training on us. I never found out if they managed to lock on to me or not, but what a great sense of achievement if they couldn't, on the other hand, it shows how good the pilots and the helicopters are if they did.

On our last drive before test day, it was a really hot day and the air-conditioning was not working, so whenever our speeds were high we had to have the windows shut due to noise and the turbulent air it caused.

The instructor was really struggling with the heat, we had already taken our ties off and undone the top buttons of our shirt, but it was still very hot and very uncomfortable. We pulled into a petrol station so he could get a cold drink and I thought it would be extremely funny to turn his heated seat on to full and leave it on. He got back in the car and off we went, completely unaware of my "prank," well, after a few miles, he was sweating, fidgeting and really cursing the weather, I was trying so hard to contain myself but eventually cracked and started to laugh at him, I had tears running down my face and our car had gone from well over 100mph to now crawling along, he then saw the light on the heated seat switch, and the number of profanities that exited his mouth was brilliant! I did feel a tad bad the next day when he had called in sick suffering with diarrhoea though!!

I love the Driver Training Unit, they are a really good bunch of seasoned and retired officers and as with all Police, need to have a laugh and love a good joke.

The final day was the test drive with the chief instructor and I passed this with no worries, I was now one of the top 5% of Police drivers in the UK and I received my certificate which my living room wall wears with pride to this day. From here on I could drive the Roads Policing vehicles, and boy was that a good feeling.

On my first duty afterwards I was allocated my vehicle, a 2006 Police spec Volvo V70 T5, this had front wheel drive, a manual gearbox, a 5 cylinder 256 bhp turbo driven engine which produced 258lb per ft. torque, punching it from 0-62mph in 6.4 seconds and had a top speed of 155mph[6], its call sign was E5G (Echo Five Golf), when you accelerated rapidly the growl of the engine and the resulting torque steer made it an exciting vehicle to drive. I was thrilled, yes it wasn't the newest or best car on the fleet, but I was new to the dept. and accepted I needed to build my experience, knowledge and respect, before I got the newer cars.

© Jeremy H Cohen. E5G in all her glory. Taken in the summer of 2010 near the junction of Holly Road and Offton Road, Offton Suffolk.

As part of my patrol, I made sure to do two things. Firstly, to drive into the town of Ipswich, there, I would drive past a building called the Willis building. This is a large office building, close to the centre of town, its exterior walls are made up of dark smoked glass panels, and yes this is a bit sad, but I drove slowly passed it admiring the reflection of the RP car I was now driving, I felt fantastic and really proud of myself.

From there, I would drive over a bridge called the Orwell Bridge. An incident hotspot for the Dept. due to the number collisions, broken down vehicles, suicides and attempted suicides. Whilst driving over the bridge I used the vehicle's radio and made a call to my wife, telling her I am now driving my own RP car. Whether she found it as exciting as I did I don't know, but hey.

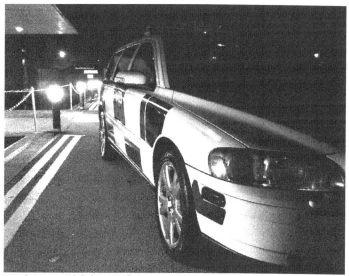

© Jeremy H Cohen. E5G Posing outside the Police HQ reception at Martlesham.

The next couple of weeks if I'm honest, was driving around going to really busy places and generally showing off my car, luckily, the siren on this one was the loudest and crispest sounding on the fleet, so it was quite easy to attract peoples' attention! As my then brother-in-law-to-be found out whilst walking his dog in the village of Hitcham!!!

With few specialist skills at this point, my time was dedicated to responding to collisions, clearing broken down vehicles and debris and conducting speed checks.

This car had a piece of kit in it that enabled speed detection of other road users when the police vehicle was both moving on a road or stationary so I quite quickly became well known for the volume of tickets I had issued.

I had a little loop I would often use and it was very productive, on a road named the A14 which was a national speed limit multi-lane carriageway, 70mph for cars, 60mph for light goods vehicles, and at the time 50mph for articulated goods vehicles. I would sit at the westbound on-slip to the carriageway, starting at junction 54. A vehicle would pass and I'd capture their speed (I concentrated on cars, motorbikes and light goods vehicles as the heavies were limited to 56mph so wasn't worth the bother), if the road surface was dry and visibility was clear I would target cars once they hit 90mph and light goods vehicles at 80mph, 20mph over their respective limits. If the weather, traffic or road conditions were worse, then that personal threshold was dropped.

I personally, did not see any need to target those motorists only 10mph over the limit, which was petty in my opinion and only caused the public to dislike Police even more. After all, speed alone cannot be deemed careless/reckless, if the road and weather conditions are fine and the driver safe, it is merely speeding. Other factors are needed to warrant it to be called careless or reckless, such as poor weather, traffic volume, the manner of driving, control of the vehicle, vehicle condition etc. etc.

In law, the Police are exempt from speed limits if adhering to that limit would hinder them from completing whatever lawful task they were doing, and no, they do not have to have blue lights flashing!!! It is the role of being a police officer, which gives the exemption. They are not however exempt from careless/reckless driving and must drive to a good standard at all times, including at high speed, so if speed alone could be careless/reckless then every Police officer, ambulance driver, fire officer, bomb disposal officer and coastguard officer would be prosecutable for careless/reckless driving every single time they sped greater than the limit. I wanted to target those that made a conscious decision to not only break the speed limit but to know they were well over it. Even with this high threshold, it was not hard to capture at least 10-15 motorists in amongst dealing with all the other incidents (usually about 10 grade "A" events) during the shift.

From this starting location, I would look to stop the offending motorist at junction 53, which was a few miles up the road or if the speeds were very high then junction 52, a bit further up. Once dealt with I would go to junction 54 but this time facing eastbound, from here I'd look to stop people at junction 55 before going back to my starting position, a nice little loop.

The straights on this section were known to the Police as the "Golden Mile." It was easy and common to capture speeds in excess of 100mph, my highest capture on that section was 122mph, and whilst on the subject, my highest capture for a 30mph zone was 83mph, also with a severely bald tyre. That was a young lad/idiot.

The other offence that I targeted at the beginning and continued to my whole service was those using a mobile phone whilst driving. It does distract and it does aid in the cause of creating collisions, some minor and some fatal. I have seen first-hand the utter destruction that a mobile phone can cause in a vehicle when the driver makes a decision to interact with it.

Owing to having few specialist skills at this point, it was not long before I felt the need and desire for more training, and greater skills to widen my capabilities. I was sure to work hard and get noticed, in the hope that when new courses came up I may be considered for them.

One of the courses I really wanted was the pursuit bronze commander's course. At the moment I could pursue a motorist, but had to give way to a fully trained officer and could not make any decisions regarding the control of and the tactical resolution of a pursuit. My fingers were crossed a course would come up soon!

Working on the major roads was without a doubt very dangerous, dealing with motorists, moving debris, everything you did required the utmost attention. So much so that many of the firearms officers that would later join our dept. did not like doing it and even said it scared them way more than anything they would have to do in the firearms role. Having 2 ton and greater, 70mph plus, missiles head towards you and sometimes passing within feet was a real eye-opener. Due to this, it was a requirement that everyone within my dept. had to be trained specifically for dealing with incidents on the "fast roads."

This training was given on an airbase and then put into practice on the roads, and if we were deemed safe then that course was complete and a certificate was presented.

A few of the simple, but very valuable things we learnt how to do properly, were;

A rolling roadblock; easily the most used safety procedure for dealing with incidents. This has usually been used when you as a motorist join a queue of unexpected really slow traffic and a few minutes later you move on with no obvious sign of why traffic had ever slowed. Whilst it may seem simple more thought went into these than appeared.

A common example of it being put to use, you attend a dual carriageway or motorway for an incident, be it debris, a broken down vehicle or a collision, and the traffic is still flowing at a decent pace. In order to stop your car, get out and deal with the incident safely, a safe zone needed to be created. It also prevented a member of the public careering blindly into whatever the hazard was.

You could on occasion begin a block up to a mile before the incident, but it all depended on the volume of traffic. You needed to create a buffer to prevent anyone harming you and also, slow traffic gradually enough to prevent people from steaming at 70mph into the back of the queue you were now building, causing another incident. Starting at the pace of other vehicles you would activate the rear facing emergency lights and straddle both lanes, preventing traffic from passing, we also lit the rear matrix signs in our vehicles, showing "DO NOT PASS" but as always, 1 or 2 idiots would sometimes try, so I would do a momentary weave, if this did not work then forcing them towards the central barrier always did!

You would then slowly decrease your speed and therefore safely slow the trailing traffic from 70mph to a crawl, when close enough to the incident, if it was safe for motorists to pass you'd take up position in the lane of the hazard and filter others into the other lane, you could then deal safely. Alternatively, if the road was unpassable due to danger, hazard or evidence, then a complete stop and block of the road would be implemented.

Sometimes we would do a rolling block following a report of an incident but when we got there nothing could be found, the RP car would then accelerate away sharply and disappear, allowing the bunched up pack to get back up to speed easily. A good example of this being done wrong was when the control room staff tried to use local

Officers with no extra training for incidents which the Road Policing Unit should be attending.

The dispatcher asked an Officer *"are you fast roads trained?"* the officer replied *"Kind of,"* already they should have come to us!!!! The Officer attended a broken down vehicle, put a rolling roadblock on and then within a few seconds was heard screaming down the radio *"Priority! Priority! There's been a crash!"* What had happened was this; the officer had joined the road and with traffic doing 70mph, took up a central position and then slammed on the brakes, causing a motorcyclist to career into the back of a sharply braking car!

Lane closures; traffic for whatever reason needed to be directed into one lane or another, or to be directed off the carriageway altogether. We would start with the rolling roadblock, then at about 900 metres away put 2 signs out, one on the central barrier and one on the verge with an instruction for the motorist to follow i.e. left arrow, road closed, slow, accident etc.… then at 600 metres and 300 metres we would repeat this. We would then use the traffic cones tapered at 30 pace intervals to gradually push traffic over into the required lane, utilising more signs amongst it.

As a final indicator, our marked vehicle with the Battenberg design on the sides would then be parked within the coned area also pointing in the direction of intended traffic flow. Done well, it looks good and is very effective at getting a motorist who may not be paying full attention to do what we required of them. Utilising the overhead electronic signs was also an added bonus, but only if you could remember to contact the Highways agency.

On a really hot day, wearing full armour and hi-vis jackets it was damn hot and sweaty work, and we'd not even dealt with the actual incident, all of this was done to prevent that one idiot who does not observe properly whilst driving from mowing us and anybody else at the scene down and smearing us over metres of the road surface.

The British police have a relatively low number of Officers killed on these very busy and fast roads, mainly down to the training given and measures taken to protect ourselves. I'd rather a bit more work and be able to walk at the end of the day than "risk it" by a complete lack of safety measures put in place. As I see it, my own life is more important than issuing a ticket, removing debris and fending off from a crash. I did whatever was needed to preserve it.

I once saw a civilian member of staff try to direct traffic on a 70 mph road by pulling his unmarked van over to the verge and then jump out into a live lane of traffic whilst wearing dark clothing, where he then pointed his hand and arm to get people hurtling towards him to move over, he was what is known as a Bell-end! He was soon stopped and I told him to leave the carriageway immediately before he is killed or another motorist is killed due to his incompetent actions. He wasn't best pleased but incompetence and a lack of common sense will eventually get you killed in this environment.

There was a lot more we went over, but unless you are a real Roads Policing geek it isn't much fun to read about. So we'll end it there.

Police officers get very good at closing off emotions and appearing 'cold' and very matter of fact when dealing with or talking about things that have happened. Sometimes though, we are only human, we freeze, we cry, we feel disabled with fear and anticipation and we are very critical of others and ourselves, sometimes holding decisions made in a split second against ourselves for all of time.

During a nice hot summer's day, I was patrolling the major roads, stopping dodgy looking vehicles and generally going about my day as usual. A call came in, a single vehicle collision on a 70mph dual carriageway, the vehicle had left the road and the occupants were not moving.

I got dispatched to attend along with some other colleagues, I, however, was only about 10 minutes away and they were some distance off. As I arrived in the vicinity, traffic was flowing steadily which I found surprising, I put on a rolling roadblock and approached the location given, with a clear road now ahead of me I began to see a vehicle up against a tree on the left verge, only inches from the road and a group of people were standing about 10 metres from it, I couldn't see much other than that yet.

I pulled to the left lane and blocked it off. Traffic started to flow past in the right-hand lane safely away from the crashed vehicle.

I got my medic box and camera out and approached the vehicle, as I drew closer I could make out the front door was open and there was a person motionless in the front seat, another also motionless person was sat on top of them, but lent over with their head hanging out of the door opening. This person was very small framed and had long blond hair, it looked like a young girl. I then got hit by what felt like a cannonball with the image of my daughter, the same colour and length of hair, it knocked me for six.

I got closer and could then make out it was actually a young boy with long hair. In the back of the car, another person was screaming and shouting, it was deafening and ear piercing, this person had been partially ejected out of the back window, half in the car and half out. The persons head and face were bleeding badly and a torn top was revealing the huge bleeding lacerations down their chest and stomach caused by the force of being ejected through the glass.

The members of public all rushed over to me in a frenzy and were shouting in horror to me, I couldn't make anything they were saying out it was all high pitched squealing.

With the injured person screeching at the top of their lungs, traffic noise flying past, the entire group of people yelling at me wanting me to sort this out, and with me all alone, I can only describe the feeling as being stuck in the centre of a tornado, but instead of wind it was loud inaudible noise racing round and round my head, disabling every aspect of my brain with a loud white noise and vibrating in my eardrums. This was the 1st very fatal collision I had attended as first on the scene. I had thousands of thoughts rushing through my mind and I had only been here for about 30 seconds and I couldn't string two thoughts together with all of the noise.

I now have to admit I lost it a bit, I yelled at the bystanders *"WILL YOU ALL JUST FUCK OFF OVER THERE!"* pointing to the verge. I know it wasn't very professional but I was ready to implode. And to those members of the public, I apologise from the bottom of my heart, for all I know this may have been the very first car crash they had seen. With the people out of my way and the noise somewhat controlled, I then got to the two people in the front of the car who were motionless, not visibly breathing and were pale in colour. Neither were moving, breathing or responding to pressure put onto the eyeball. I could see that the vehicle had gone broadside into a tree, bending the car literally like a banana, the two front occupants were on top of each other because the force of the collision had actually pushed the front seats on top of each other, creating a single seat width vehicle.

I then made a decision that to this day still haunts me, I had to prioritise a victim, the person in the rear, although alive and screaming was gushing thick internal blood and had muscle hanging from the deep tears to their chest and stomach, he was going to die. I believed from what I had seen and felt that the 2 front occupants were well and truly dead and I, therefore, chose to help the rear passenger and I gave no further help to those in the front, other than instructing the bystanders to get them out and onto the ground, whilst I tried to save the rear persons life.

With no bandages big enough for a torso wrap, I took off my jacket and held it as hard as I could across the torso of this person trying to prevent them from bleeding out and dying.

Luckily, within no more than a minute, a fast response paramedic had arrived. The paramedic checked on the front two and said they were, in fact, dead, and then came to help me with my person.

My colleagues arrived shortly after the paramedic and the road got completely shut down and things dramatically calmed down.

The rear passenger thankfully survived from what I had been told were life-threatening injuries, ones which I had acted to help with. This passenger in the future, would go on to say the driver had reached for a mobile phone, causing a momentary drift of the car which then led it in to the gravel drain along the edge of the road, the driver then tried to correct the vehicle but it resulted in a total loss of control and the vehicle leaving the road to impact with a tree.

I spoke with the paramedic and they tried to reassure me the front occupants would almost certainly have been dead well before I had arrived, but the lack of help I could give them cycles my mind like a bad cloud constantly present in my life, I couldn't save one of them.

This incident would leave me battling PTSD (Post Traumatic Stress Disorder) for a while after and to this day I still suffer from one single side effect; I hate with great passion, shouting and screeching right next to my head, it creates that feeling of the tornado of noise I had at this collision, I can't think or comprehend anything and it feels like the noise is strangling my brain. The downside to having kids is a lot of loud shouting and screaming and that, in turn, makes me tell them off a fair bit! I hope when they are old enough to read and appreciate what is written in this book, that they see I didn't mean to a complete tyrant.

After a while of dealing with numerous amounts of crashes, tickets and prosecutions I was given my pursuit commanders course. This would be a huge patch on my arm if I could pass it, but could also see me kicked off the dept. if I failed.

A group totalling six people from my department were on the course, two per car plus an instructor. Another instructor would also be the driver of a bandit vehicle which we would be chasing down and stopping.

We spent a couple of days up at the airbase again, this time we were practising the stopping tactics used to stop and disable a vehicle that we were pursuing.

Whilst you can watch Police pursuits on the TV and see Police perform a "box" on a high-speed vehicle or use tactical contact in different situations, the discussion of tactics and how to create or force a situation to use those tactics tend to be kept from the public, and I am not changing that.

I still believe the Police should be able to chase and stop offenders who decide to flee, and the greater the advantage is with the Police, the less risk is afforded to them, the public and also the fleeing motorist. For that reason, I will not go into how a tactic can be implemented and planned. But I will tell you that learning them is awesome fun!!!!!!!

We spent time spinning cars out, driving over 100mph with body panels rubbing against each other, making split-second decisions at high speed and also how to get our vehicle away from a serious threat to ourselves. We would then conduct mock pursuits chasing the instructor on the public roads. I can remember a few times the public tried to help out, thinking we were involved in a live pursuit.

One particular incident was when we were chasing on the A14 and an articulated goods vehicle driver, upon seeing us in his mirrors, decided to suddenly swing his vehicle violently across the road into the path of the instructor who was trying to flee from us. The instructor was in an unmarked vehicle, so it was not immediately evident it was actually the Police. The instructor had to swerve and skid to a stop by the central barrier, the goods vehicle driver seeing this got out and went to chase him! Seeing this unfold we got over to him quickly and "arrested" the instructor (to keep the public from knowing we were conducting high-risk training on the roads). The look on the instructor's face was one of such relief when we got to him, it was priceless.

We got used to using vehicle trackers, the stinger and the helicopter during our training as ways of assisting us in safely resolving a pursuit.

The instructor who acted as the bandit, was well known to us all for sometimes going a bit too far in an attempt at creating realism, which created some moments of fun. A few incidents stuck out in my mind from the training.

On one occasion I was pursuing him along a single track lane, I had arranged for the end tactic to be implemented just a few bends ahead, we flew along this single vehicle width lane and then he broke extremely hard, he had just caught a glimpse of another police vehicle just ahead and waiting. He slammed it into reverse and with that my in-car instructor then adds to the equation *"the bandit is armed, get away."* I slammed on the brakes and got reverse, going backwards down the twisty country lane, the revs bouncing at the max and the engine screaming out at the top of its range took some major concentration, but was a great buzz.

The next incident was this; his vehicle had been stung (gone over the stinger – a tyre deflation device with sets of hollow spikes) and I was waiting around the next bend to stop his slowing vehicle. He came round the bend, then tried to force past us, my in-car instructor was not happy the bandit hadn't then taken that as the cue to stop and yelled at me *"JUST BLOODY STOP HIM!"* I only needed telling once, with the bandit car trying to push past me I forced back towards him and pushed him into the ditch, that stopped him! I thought that the training being this realistic was and is still, in my opinion, the only way to train. Train for reality, then reality is the norm.

During our course there was a day the control room Inspectors would come out and observe us from within our cars, this was done so they knew what training we had done and when we were speaking of different tactics they could visualise what we were planning and the various risks associated with each. A valuable day for them in my opinion, but one Inspector who had only ever been trained as a standard response driver and didn't like speed gave up halfway through the day, it was too much for him!

Following the successful conclusion of the course, I was now a qualified Police Pursuit Bronze commander. I could now decide upon which tactic and when/how to implement it in an attempt to stop and disable a fleeing vehicle. A position that was well respected and one where the commander had authority over any ranking officer in the decision-making process of an authorised pursuit.

The authorisation of pursuits, when it is apparent a vehicle is failing to stop for Police, that fact is relayed to the control room Inspector, they are made aware of the reason for the initial request to stop, the weather, road conditions, and your driving authorisation level. Based on the information given, a pursuit would be authorised and therefore granted the commander the open book of tactics, except for a couple of the tactics which required further authorisation, they were ones that would likely kill the suspect. Alternatively, the Inspector would say the pursuit is not authorised. An example of a good reason for not authorising could be, an initial stop for just a light out with no other intelligence on the vehicle or occupants, you're in the proximity of schools at kicking out time, being a non-pursuit driver and it is raining heavily. My shift had a control room Inspector that was brilliant, he knew the law very well and had a great deal of respect for the things we did and for training we had received.

A very important aspect of this commander entitlement was not only being able to chase people and use tactics to stop them, but also to have the presence of mind to continually assess the driving of the bandit vehicle, if it got too dangerous or put people at risk unnecessarily we would call off the pursuit.

I honestly believe Policing is a risky business and sometimes that risk is needed to achieve the policing goals of catching and deterring criminals. Is there a need to chase a person, at 90mph in residential streets running red lights and swerving around other road users and pedestrians if you believe the only offence is not wearing a seat belt??? I don't think so. If the offence is more serious or further information is available then things should be judged differently. Sometimes you have no idea why they are fleeing, and if it was only for a documents check that you requested a stop, again where do you draw the line. On the other end of the scale, if you have a known murderer or terror cell, then the risk to the public should be weighed against the risk to the community as a whole, risk a few to save many.

Pursuing may appear a glamorous side of policing and fun on the TV, but the reality of it is this; every decision you make as the pursuing officer can haunt you, if through your actions or lack of actions an innocent member of the public is killed or injured, even if solely down to the actions of the fleeing motorist, you will be scrutinised beyond belief, and with the British courts becoming increasingly likely to hold cases against Officers involved in pursuits resulting in injuries, months of worry lay ahead of you and your family.

The saying *"With great power comes great responsibility"* is very true. It is, for this reason, I would soon get a name for myself as one that would smash into the fleeing vehicles to stop a pursuit and end the risk to the public at the first opportunity I got. Sometimes it would work, sometimes not, but if anyone ever scrutinised my pursuits they would see I tried at every given opportunity to stop it.

In the environment I now worked in, pursuits occurred relatively often, 2-3 times a week and sometimes, depending on the days tasking's 2-3 in a day.

The opportunity to utilise my new found skills wouldn't have to wait long.

It was late evening and starting to get dark, I was out in a small rural village conducting speed checks in a 30mph zone. The previous few nights had seen a number of burglaries in the area and I was hoping to help put a stop to it. A small dark coloured hatchback passed me at over 50mph. I pulled out to stop the vehicle and it appeared to have only one occupant (in the police, a term called 1 up). I activated my emergency equipment, lights and siren, gave it a good headlight flash and indicated to the left for the vehicle to pull over, the vehicle slowed and pulled to the side of the road, but before it got to a complete stop it then accelerated away from my now slowing patrol vehicle, I was now into a pursuit. I broadcast this fact to the operations room, confirmed my driver training level and pursuit commander status, the pursuit was immediately authorised.

We travelled the twisty country roads for about 10 minutes, before the fleeing vehicle, unable to shake the power of my car realised this and the driver then chose to enter woodland, being a small agile car in a confined area of trees, the driver may have hoped I'd give up or be unable to stay with him. Speeds through the trees were only 30mph or so, we were not on any kind of track just a grassy woodland floor, dodging the trees as we went, it was not going as planned for him, he hadn't lost me, he then went into an area of tighter lined trees and squeezed through a much tighter gap. Knowing my vehicle was larger, I knew it would be tight, the only way I could get through was by sacrificing the cosmetics of my car, what the heck, it's only a tool! I aimed centrally and went for it, the good news is it only smashed off the side mirrors, and I was still in the hunt! Albeit the gap had grown a bit now.

We exited the woods and were back onto the paved country roads, the advantage was back with me, the driver then made a surprising turn that took him towards a local military airbase on a one-way road, thinking he'll have to stop soon I was feeling confident. As we approached the black gates to the airbase, I thought he was going way to fast to stop at the gate, he was going to go straight through them I thought. Seeing the armed guards at the gate I drew back, allowing them room to fire upon the car hurtling towards them, but they did not! He screamed past the guards and dodged the gate, continuing on to the base.

I was in utter shock, who is this???? Now off the public roads and in a much safer environment, I used the performance of my vehicle to get right on him and end this debacle right now! Knowing what needed to be done, I drew to the side of him, then planted the front end of my vehicle into his passenger side door, and pushed him into a low concrete wall, stopping him dead, in a moment of *"fuck you!"* I got out and dragged him from his car and planted him on the floor, handcuffed him and I remember saying *"that didn't go well did it!"* to him.

I was shortly joined by military personnel who assisted me until another Police unit arrived to take him to custody.

During the upcoming investigation, it transpired, he was uninsured, unlicensed and had a load of illegally possessed knives in his vehicle. He was also a member of the military and was based where I had stopped him. I, therefore, took great pride in calling and waking the Commanding officer of the base up, who then personally made a trip to the Police custody to collect the chap, at 3 am! He was not at all happy!!! As most of the area could hear!

The criminals of Suffolk at this time were not used to Police ramming (using tactical contact) against them, there had always been an *"I don't want to damage a police car"* mentality, and I remember one pursuit for that very reason.

I was on the night shift double crewed, there had been a number of burglaries at a few remote farms in the county. A call then came in reporting a van had entered a farm and the occupants were stealing diesel from the farms' tanks, I responded to the area, arriving about 5-10 minutes after the call. The call was still ongoing as we arrived in the area, and we received regular commentary on what was happening. Before we got to the actual premises the van had left, we had a description of what to look for, so this should be easy! Low and behold about a minute later a van matching the same description came towards us, 2 up, and accelerated past, I turned around and gave chase, he was heading back towards the town of Ipswich, about 8 miles away.

The fleeing driver was being very kind and was actually using his indicators when turning, which I thought was priceless! Anyway, the van could only get to about 80-90mph, but at that speed and for that level of offence I was not going to take him off the road just yet, I did, however, have my plan. We had gotten onto the A14 and utilising another Police vehicle, we used a tactic to prevent it from leaving at any of the junctions.

When we got to the junction I wanted for my resolution, using the other Police vehicle we forced the van to take this junction. We got a mile down the road and the van was presented with a large grassed area with trees, and also a dead end. Trying to double back he mounted the grass, as did I, perfect! As he started to perform a U-turn I parked the nose of my car nice and hard into side of the van and pushed it into a tree, pinning it there unable to move, I can remember an occupant looking out the side window seeing my car impacted in to his door and a look of *"what the fuck?"* on his face. I loved it. I wasn't one for pussyfooting around and soon got the nickname of 'maverick' off a couple of officers, although my long-serving and the most common nickname was "G" or G Star."

Unfortunately, the official tactics didn't work every time and sometimes we had to rely on the fleeing driver being unable to maintain high speeds and stressful driving for longer periods of time and would then crash out. As a department we drove at high speeds every day, with high risk and high stresses being an everyday part of the job, it honestly felt like you could start knitting at 120mph because we were so used to it.

Again a night shift, I was double-crewed and also had the Armed Response Vehicle (ARV), to the Americans – SWAT but in a fast car, accompanying me. There had been a residential burglary, and a vehicle had been seen.

We went out hunting for it, trawling the back streets and rat runs through the estates and it was not long before I was confronted with a similar looking vehicle coming towards me. As it drew much closer the headlights went onto full beam, momentarily obstructing my view of the driver, it then fled past me, I turned and gave chase.

Through the quiet residential streets at 2 am, the ARV was at this point the lead vehicle, the fleeing car kept slamming on their brakes and reversing at them, this happened 3 or 4 times. The next time it did it, I shot out from behind the ARV to overtake, and seeing a parked car to the side of the road, which was unoccupied, I quickly formulated that I would stove into the fleeing car, and push it into the parked car, and with the ARV driver also being a fully trained pursuit officer, I knew they would then cover the rear of the car, giving it no escape.

So, speeds were now only 20-25mph as it had just broken hard again, I'd pulled out, overtook and drew alongside the fleeing vehicle and then dynamically put the nose of my vehicle into the side door of the fleeing car and pushed it. He too was pushing back against me, and just before being slammed into the parked car, it managed to squirm past me and started off down the road.

We again gave chase, this time with me as lead vehicle, we continued for about 5 minutes in the outskirts of the town, hitting speeds of 80-90mph, then headed out of town towards the A14. As we got there, we were not close enough to prevent an act of utter stupidity, but the fleeing vehicle drove up on to this 70mph road and drove the wrong way down it, into the oncoming traffic. Had we been closer, we would have had no hesitation in hitting the fleeing car as hard as we could, barrel rolling it away from the area, yes it would risk very serious injury to the occupants but could save the lives of innocent road users it would now be driving head on towards at over 70mph.

We killed all of our emergency equipment and joined the carriageway the correct way to monitor his actions, we will not drive the wrong way down a 70mph road unless it is an extremely serious threat where the lives of a few members the public were justifiably put at risk to save a lot (think of a bomber with the capacity and intent to kill 100's of people).

We saw the car narrowly avoid a head-on collision with an articulated goods vehicle and then it left the road and headed towards a truck stop. We were now back in the chase. It approached a railroad crossing and drove straight through the metal track gate knocking it off its hinges, and it was left lying on the tracks, we obviously stopped to remove this hazard to any approaching train. By this time the vehicle had now left our sights, we chose a direction and continued on. We found the vehicle crashed about a mile further up the road, it had hit a speed limit sign whilst trying to make a left turn and this had disabled his vehicle and now nobody was with it. The Police helicopter and dog unit were called to help, unfortunately, they were never found. But, proof of what I was saying, they could not continue for too long before their driving skill and experience would catch up with them resulting in a crash.

It was not long until I starting using the next Roads Policing car of my career, the old E5G with high mileage was now retiring, having served her duty well.

Next came the use of E5E, a 2009 Police Spec Volvo V70 T6, this vehicle had All Wheel Drive and a 3.0litre 6 cylinder engine. An animal with over 280 horses powered through a supercharged turbo driven engine, using a 6-speed Tiptronic gearbox and 325lb per ft. torque it achieved 0-62mph in 6.5 seconds and was limited to 155mph[7]

© Jeremy H Cohen. E5E taken at the entrance to 'Suffolk Farmhouse
Cheeses' just off the A140 at Creeting St Peter.

© Jeremy H Cohen. E5E's sister vehicle E5D, Taken somewhere near the
B1078/9 Clopton, the precise location I cannot remember.

Although on paper this was a very similar car in performance stats, it did, however, knock my old T5 E5G out to pasture. With the uprated braking, suspension and the additions of the All-Wheel Drive system and a Tiptronic gearbox, you could make this thing fly and maintain a much higher average speed!

It could hold greater speeds in the corners, had hell of a strong brakes, had no torque steering issues, and with a more elevated driving position, it allowed you to have much greater confidence in pushing it that bit more than the T5. A great advancement was it could turn on a dime, whereas the old T5 was like turning the Titanic around, and best of all it had the CD player and radio left in it, and let me tell you, there was nothing quite like a warm clear summers day, thundering along with the Top Gun anthem playing! It was brilliant.

I noticed a difference with the criminals as well, for a while they gave up on pursuits, if this thing showed up, with a trained RP Officer at the wheel, they knew it would be much harder to flee from, but the downside was that criminals eventually started to steal and use higher powered vehicles than previously, knowing they too needed a new piece of kit to match us. The pursuits then started up again.

I remember one night a quote from a well-known little shit that was a burglar and active in vehicle crime.

I was out in the quiet villages hunting for ne'er-do-wells, and was sat hidden, backed down in a dark lane, watching what went past. A small hot hatch passed me and it gave me that feeling of, *"that needs stopping!"* Out I went and soon I got behind it, I could see the vehicle was 3 up and there was a lot of activity going on in the car, with the passengers repeatedly turning to look at me. I lit the car up and it pulled over, the driver immediately got out and to my surprise, it was this shit that I knew, normally he would try and flee, this surprised me so much that I even said to him, *"That was easier than normal."* I distinctly remember him replying, *"no point in trying against you guys in those!"* pointing at my car. Well, they all got searched including the car and nothing was found enabling any arrests, but plenty of information was obtained for a decent Intel submission and they also now knew this area was out of bounds. I hopefully saved someone from being burgled that night.

In 2012, London, England, played host to the Olympic Games. A moment in world history that I was able to get slightly involved with.

As you will know, just prior to the Games the Olympic torch is carried by bearers the world over until it finally arrives to light the fire of the games.

On July 5th 2012, the torch was carried under a heavy media spotlight through the streets of Suffolk. It was under Police and officials escort and crowds formed by members of the public lined the streets to watch it pass. Little did people know, but running parallel to the torch and procession, but out of sight of the public and cameras was a team of officers, covering the many security and safety disciplines imaginable. There was bomb experts, hazardous chemical experts, quick strike teams ready to go in, arrest and get out anyone causing major problems or threatening the safety of those involved or spectating, and riot police.

I, owing to my driver training level, had the job of being the driver for one of the quick strike teams, a job that sounds great, but thankfully nothing happened and we shadowed the torch until it had completed the long tour of the county. A moment though that gained me a commemorative coin from the then Prime Minister David Cameron, with a signed insert that reads, *"Please accept this commemorative medallion as a symbol of our gratitude for your efforts in helping deliver the safe and secure London 2012 Games. Thank you for a job well done and be proud of your contribution to this spectacular moment in our history."* These were issued to Police Officers and Military personnel engaged in the security operation.

I briefly mentioned earlier a place named the Orwell Bridge, this was a huge bridge, well 2 bridges actually, side by side which was part of the A14 dual carriageway. It had an air gap of over 140 feet in height and was close to a mile in length. It was a dual carriageway subjected to a 70mph speed limit, which would later be reduced to 60mph with the addition of fixed average speed cameras in an attempt at increasing safety and cutting the volume of incidents occurring on it.

There was a footpath running over it on both sides of the road and a parapet wall about 3 feet in height and one foot thick. It was the main way for commuters to get from one side of the River Orwell to the other on the A14 and any incident always created absolute bedlam for the town of Ipswich and other surrounding villages.

Most days, we as a department were called there, it was a suicide hotspot for the county, there were numerous broken down vehicles and numerous collisions that all required our attendance. I would often joke when I left the Unit to begin my patrols, *"See you on the Bridge"* I'd say. And it wasn't often wrong.

One surprising skill I acquired working for the Roads Policing Unit was that of talking to and negotiating with suicidal people. I cannot count the number of times I attended this bridge to talk someone down from the parapet or to search for a body on the fields and river banks below, but not many weeks passed without the need for me to do so. Most of the time it resulted in the compliant removal of someone and then sectioning them under section 136 of the Mental Health Act, and removing them from the public place to a mental health hospital.

At this bridge I saw the damage caused to a humans body after a fall from that height, it was not pretty and always made me wonder how bad things must be in someone's mind to actually enable them to launch off a bridge knowing the resulting fall would kill them. Apart from once….

I was on a night shift and was dispatched to the bridge following a call from a truck driver, who had driven onto the bridge and crashed into a van, which was stationary at the very top of it, he also could not find the driver anywhere. My initial thought was someone had broken down and walked off for help, it always amazed me but with no shoulder to this section of road, some idiots would run out of fuel and just ditch their vehicle whilst they went for more fuel, often not even notifying the Police.

I arrived, and indeed found the truck with front end damage and a van with substantial rear damage as had been reported. I then walked to the van in the hope of finding a note or some contact details for the driver and as I was walking, I heard someone calling out very faintly. I grabbed my light, and shone it over the edge of the bridge and down onto the water below, with this, the calling became more persistent and clearer, *"HELP!" "HELP!"* and there in the river below was a man floating away with the current. That was a total shock to me, I'd never known anyone to survive that fall.

Coastguard was called and the man was picked out of the water and taken to the hospital. It was confirmed he had gone to the bridge, stopped at the top and jumped straight over the wall intent on killing himself, and even more surprising to me was the fact he only suffered a bruised liver! He obviously wasn't meant to die.

Most of the time we got called there, it was from a passing motorist who had seen someone on the parapet or had seen someone disappear off the edge. I had two days in a row where I had to attend the bridge for suicidal people that I will always remember above the rest.

Firstly; we had a call about a young female sitting on the wall with her feet and legs hanging over the edge. I was sent to deal with this along with another unit, but they were some way off.

Whenever I arrived, I always put in a rolling roadblock and completely stopped the traffic, this gave me a safe and sterile area to deal with the person and made room for me to deal with any sudden attempts to run in front of a moving vehicle. In an ideal world, we would try and stop both directions but it was not always possible due to staffing and other incidents.

As I pulled up I could see the young lady sitting on the wall, I called out and she totally ignored me, she didn't even glance my way. I slowly approached asking her questions as I went, trying to engage her in conversation, trying to draw her attention away from the reason she was there.

When I was about 5 metres away I saw her posture quickly change, she launched herself forwards and off of the wall, towards her death. I somehow made up the remaining ground in a blink of an eye, with her body now disappearing and then her wrists disappearing from view, I reached out and grabbed them, holding her wrists as tight as I possibly could. She was now hanging 140 feet from the ground with only me stopping her fall, and to compound matters she then started tugging her weight down by repeatedly bending her legs and dropping them, making it even harder to hold her. With the course sharp stoned parapet wall digging and cutting into my arms I knew I could not lift her over myself. After a while, I came to the realisation I had been battling so hard against, she would have to fall, I could not keep hold of her in this stalemate for much longer.

I was getting weaker and weaker, finally one of her hands became free, I quickly put my free hand to her other wrist, my two hands were now holding one wrist, my muscles were shaking, sweat was pouring from my face and my hands were becoming increasingly clammy, I couldn't let her go! Having my arms resting on the top of the wall was helping a lot but my wrists and forearms were giving up!

My attention was then drawn to a field below, a village fete was ongoing, and the crew from a fire engine must have seen what was happening and drove over and stopped, now underneath us. *What can they do? This is too high for any ladder or platform!* I then felt the pressure of someone else against my side, a colleague had arrived, he took hold of her arm and together we dragged her back up and over the wall, causing some serious cuts to her stomach, but her heart was still beating which was the main aim of all this.

She was detained and taken away and I was left amazed that nobody in the line of stopped traffic came to help me, but as I went back to my vehicle I could see that due to the angle of the slope they wouldn't have even known anything was going on whilst they were waiting patiently behind my car.

I later watched the footage from my cars' video and I had held that lady for just over 4 minutes, but it felt like an eternity. That was the single most exhausting thing I had ever done, even more exhausting than CPR, which is shattering. The will to hold onto someone knowing if you let go, they will die, musters an incredible amount of energy and a true testament to the power gained from adrenaline.

The very next morning I got called to the bridge again, this time, a man was seen to be running and jumping about on the bridge parapet wall!

I made my way there and some colleagues also said they would attend, but cannot do so immediately due to a commitment at the unit.

I arrived within a few minutes and as per the norm I had stopped the traffic to get the safe sterile area to work in, and to my astonishment, I did, in fact, find a young man who was running back and forth on the narrow wall.

I called out to him and he told me to *"get lost"* and said it's up to him if he kills himself. Whilst many may agree with that sentence the Police are duty bound by law to protect life and limb, so that doesn't leave the "get lost" option available.

I went up to the wall and leant against it, about 10 metres away from him and tried to engage him in conversation, but soon realised I was not getting anywhere fast. Due to the fact he was dancing on the wall and his general demeanour, I could tell he was high on drugs, I'd been around enough druggies to know! All of this time remembering I have the busiest road in the county stopped, with queues building at a mile a minute.

For no apparent reason there was a sudden personality change, he calmly got down off the wall and started to approach me, he was apparently handing himself in and wanted help to sort his issues out. Knowing I was still alone, I obviously took this with a pinch of salt. He was now extremely calm and focused. I knew that being alone with a suicidal drugged up person, on the top of a 140ft bridge that he would need to be restrained and not allowed in my vehicle without a minimum of handcuffs being applied.

After speaking to him for a further minute, he decided he would allow me to remove him from the bridge and then wait for more suitable transport to take him to the hospital. I even explained I would be needing to handcuff him to which he said that's understandable.

I took out my cuffs and as I reached forward to apply to the first wrist, he lunged with all his might and speed throwing a punch towards me, shouting *"you're going over!"*

With the cuff in my hand, I smashed him in the throat as hard as I could, knocking him to the ground. He was kicking out violently, trying to get up and constantly throwing punches my way, entangling me in his flailing limbs as he did so. I was smashing with all my might against his major nerve groups with the tip of my rigid cuffs, momentarily crippling the impacted limb, allowing me to get some time and a touch of thought process going.

At the edge of the bridge was a very narrow footpath, with a crash barrier running along it separating traffic and pedestrians, we were between the wall and barrier on the pathway, it was a small and tight arena.

As I went to step back and away from him, I stumbled forward as my foot slipped down the lip of the kerb and in turn caused my calf to hit the barrier, this made me fall forwards onto the male, he was trying to hit and grab at me as I fell.

As I landed, I rammed my forearm across his throat and held it down as hard as I could, compressing his windpipe and jugular vein, stopping him quite successfully. At this point, I did not care if it seriously affected his breathing, the thought in the back of my mind was that if he wanted to kill himself, what would stop him throwing me over the edge if he got the chance.

With the tiredness of restraining him and avoiding being struck I honestly thought to myself, *"am I going to have to kill him to save myself?"* For the most part, amongst his violent movements, I had managed to keep my forearm locked down across his throat and smother his other arm with my free arm. I luckily then had two members of the public come running over from the queue of cars to help me out. With three of us now on him, I managed to force the cuffs on to his wrists and pin him up against the wall, exhausted and out powered he had finally given up the fight.

After a few more minutes, my colleagues then arrived and we got him transported to the hospital. He was cut, bruised and now eerily quiet again.

My two colleagues and I waited with him in the hospital whilst he was checked over by a nurse for any major injuries.

I don't know how many of you have ever experienced the violence and strength from someone when high on drugs, but the amount of power they can exert is incredible. It is honestly as though that bit of our mind that holds us back and prevents us from using the full 100% of our power is momentarily gone when high on drugs, and this was evidenced in the hospital.

The male, who was about 6ft tall and of a medium build, not hugely muscular or anything, was laying on his back on the hospital bed, for some reason he then had another turn of aggression, suddenly starting to shout out and with the 3 of us holding him down on the bed and still handcuffed, he stood straight up on the bed, as though pulled by a hydraulic wire, we could barely contain him.

It was days like this that I was actually really appreciative of the close combat personal safety training we received, the days of training, trying new things out and having to escape harm and defend yourself are worth it! Having the feeling of being attacked played out on a regular basis significantly reduced the shock factor that is associated with a violent confrontation, making it less likely for you to freeze and therefore be subjected to greater harm. One thing that had stuck with me was that the forearm is a mightily powerful weapon and a hard one to overcome when used properly.

In this incident, I was extremely grateful for the members of the public being confident enough to come and assist me, as my colleagues took a while to arrive. This situation could have continued on and in that particular scenario I know I would have had to use deadly force to protect myself from what was a very real threat to my life.

This was a moment in my life that the danger wasn't fully realised until later, once the adrenaline had died down. The odd thing about Policing is I dealt with this incident and then it was on to the next, as though nothing had happened. How many people if violently attacked and had their life at risk would take the day off work or need a break? For the Police, it was a daily hazard and something that had to be moved on from. Truly a bizarre concept.

Following these two incidents on consecutive days, the supervisor at my base put me forward for an award, agreeing it was good and hard work.

Unfortunately, the award that month went to a neighbourhood Officer that had designed a new "parking enforcement" leaflet! Whatever!! The politics of Policing!

Due to the knock-on effect of issues on the Orwell Bridge, the area was constantly receiving media interest, and normally negative press, due to incidents causing delays or the sad news because of a suicide or as the press write it *"a person fell from the bridge"* Really? They didn't fall, they meant it! During my career, there was only one piece of really good, happy and joyful news from the bridge, which occurred one night shift when I was double crewed with my colleague and good friend Andy.

We were on the bridge dealing with a broken down motorist who had suffered an engine blowout and the resulting oil spill meant we couldn't just tow this one out of the way like normal, we had to close a lane in order for it to be recovered and have the oil spill cleaned away.

We had got everything in place and were waiting for the recovery truck, and whilst sat in our car chatting, we saw a car behind approach us at speed and pull into our coned off area of the lane.

If I'm really honest and frank, the Police hate it when someone out of the blue approaches them, usually a phrase like *"stupid question time"* or *"this one's yours"* is passed between the Officers, but despite this little bit of humour, the Police Officers I have met will always help no matter what the "stupid question" ends up being.

The car stopped and a man came running over, shouting as he ran, we got out and were told the man's wife was in labour and having a baby and wouldn't make it to the hospital. Right… I've seen the TV shows and films, how bad can this be!!! I went over to the car and found a young lady heavily pregnant and doing some really serious panting, this was real! She was sweating, red-faced, shouting, everything you see on "call the midwife," she definitely wouldn't make it to the hospital.

Whilst my colleague arranged for an ambulance to attend, I spoke with the lady and laid her seat back, I was calmly and clearly talking to her and she was SHOUTING responses back! I helped her get her trousers down and cover her with a blanket to add that little touch of dignity and class to the whole occasion! And within moments of playing Dr, out shoots, and I mean shoots!!! A little baby boy, all bloody and screaming. How nice this moment was, although, with cars still hurtling within feet from us at 70+ mph, it was just a tad risky! Andy then took over the care and ensured mum and baby were nice and warm whilst we waited on an ambulance, which didn't take too long to arrive.

This whole situation had happened in less than 10 minutes. It was then not long before the new mum, dad and baby were taken by ambulance to the hospital.

Andy, then realising faster than I did, that we now had their car to move, quickly bagged the driver's seat of the Police vehicle, *"bugger!"* I thought.

Once the broken down vehicle was recovered, I then had the pleasure of getting into the driver's seat of what was now a very hot car, with a miniature scale scene from any of the "Saw" franchise movies on the front passenger seat, slopping about and stinking. The hospital was about 4 miles away, so with the windows down and me gagging the whole way I delivered the car to the maternity ward, and in case you're wondering, we did then go that extra mile by cleaning up as best we could the front seat area for them.

As a force, it is an annual requirement for each front line Officer to receive initial responder first aid training (CPR, Defib, cuts, breaks, burns, diabetic issues, heart issues, head injuries etc, but not midwifery training!). Dealing with that incident which we were in no way trained for and doing so in the high-risk environment that it was, gained both my colleague and I a "Chief Constables Commendation." The even better news for me was that my wife was waiting on her start date for her Bachelor's degree in midwifery, and I had beaten her at delivering a baby! I very quickly sent her a message letting her know I had helped in a birth, her response was, *"animal or human?"* I guess she thought I got up to some weird shit!

It was really nice to see the bridge in the media telling of a happy story for once. The story filled the papers, the local news channel and the radio, I think it is brilliant that a bridge that takes so many lives has now given one back.

Helping couples during this time of great importance is a good feeling, one that warms your soul and one I can see why midwives enjoy their job.

I only ever helped out in the moments of labour one other time, but this time it was not too "involved."

During a winter snowstorm, the roads had become gridlocked and everywhere was at a crawl or total standstill, I was helping move stranded cars on the A14 and was approached by a man from a few cars down the queue.

He told me his wife was giving birth, thankfully not in quite an advanced stage as the previous account but with the slow going traffic, I knew it wouldn't be too long. I told him to drive up between the vehicles and get directly behind my car, I would then escort him on blue lights across the town to the hospital. We carved our way through the busy streets and although I never took him over 30mph, I'm sure he found it a great experience. After about 10-15 minutes I had safely delivered them to the hospital where a healthy young girl was born, what an entrance! A few weeks later I was shocked and pleasantly surprised to receive a letter from the couple thanking me for the help I gave them that evening. I have kept it to this day along with my other career keepsakes and it reminds me of the good feeling you get when you genuinely help someone in a time of need.

Helping children when subjected to the tragedy of serious crashes was something that gave you that same feeling and also made you question your own parenting techniques and responsibilities.

On a warm spring day, a vehicle had crashed off the A14 and after a roll came to rest against some trees by a steep downhill embankment. The male driver and his daughter aged about 5 had rented a car and were visiting the area. The driver had suffered serious life-threatening injuries and had multiple cuts across his face and was placed into an induced coma by the attending critical care doctor. The daughter, other than shaken and crying wasn't too bad.

I was very conscious of how the girl was going to feel, seeing her daddy covered in blood and having a lot of strangers doing all manner of things to him.

The Roads Policing vehicles at the time all carried a 'teddy bear' to give the children as a gift when involved in such cases in the hope of taking some of the drama away for them.

I gave the girl the teddy which she immediately loved to bits and I sat her down on the grass embankment, talking to her about her dad. I asked her name and age, which she told me and I then asked her dads name, again she knew it. When I asked her *"do you know where you live?"* she didn't have a clue.

That was a moment that stuck with me. I didn't want my kids being unable to give vital information to emergency service personnel if, it was ever needed. I started to teach mine their full address straight away after that.

After a long course of treatment at a specialist hospital, the driver survived.

Although having stories like these showing what the more interesting aspect of my job was, a major part of my role was to proactively hunt out traffic related infringements and all of my spare time was dedicated to this and as a result, I often get asked, *"what's the best excuses a driver gave you?"* and *"did you ever stop someone really weird?"*

Well, during my time in the Police and especially the Roads Policing Unit, I obviously stopped 1000's of vehicles and dealt with people for numerous offences or "educated" them on their behaviour. I have made an educated estimate, based on my daily average, that during my career, I conducted over 30,000 vehicle stops alone and if I'm honest only a few stick out, so I apologise if you were expecting a good laugh…

A few excuses I was given by people caught speeding;

"It's alright officer, I work for charity"
"But didn't you speed to catch me up?"
"I'm about to shit myself" and believe it or not *"I have shit myself"*
"I'm desperate for a wee"
"I'm running out of fuel and wanted to get to a fuel station"
"I didn't realise" at over 100mph, I doubt it! A Liar, pure and simple.
"I'm a Freeman and don't recognise your authority or the laws"
And one I found particularly good, which made me take even longer, was when I stopped a young lady who was very provocatively dressed who said; *"I've been at another man's house and I'm trying to get back home before my partner gets in."* Naughty! I wrote my ticket incredibly slowly for that one!!

There were other interactions that were quite interesting mind you…

One night I was following a large expensive car, we approached a roundabout and as I started to back off I realised the car ahead hadn't, it carried straight on and went up the kerb onto the raised grass roundabout and crashed into a road sign. I stopped and went over to the car, an elderly man got out of the driver's seat, clearly drunk as a skunk and staggering all over the place, he saw me and said: *"it's alright officer, I'm just picking mushrooms!"*
"Actually, you're under arrest mate!"

Then there was the time I stopped an articulated goods vehicle to examine the tachograph (a device that records the drivers driving hours). I climbed up into the cab and found an overweight middle-aged man dressed up in skimpy ladies underwear. I believe I actually brought up a little bit of sick with that one!

Another goods vehicle had broken down, causing an obstruction to the A14. Now, generally, and based on my experience, a large number of goods vehicle drivers were male, and a large proportion of them were a tad overweight. As I approached this vehicle the driver got out of the cabin and walked over to me, the driver was a young and very attractive lady wearing her gym outfit! That was a shock!

Then, as the incident progressed, I noticed other RP Officers pull up and want to help, they kept coming like ants around a sugar cube! Usually, it was a fight to get someone to help with a broken down goods vehicle, but not today. Guess this one was different!

Whilst this next example was not someone I stopped it also highlights the kind of people wandering around in society;

I was on a night shift with a colleague and we were patrolling a very rural area, seeing somewhere different to the main road for a bit. The area was very remote with only a few houses dotted about and as we passed an old large house which was set back behind some thick hedges and large trees, we heard an alarm going off. The house's burglar alarm was sounding and we decided to go take a look. With our torches out, we walked around the edge of the house, checking for any sign of a break in, then out of the darkness behind us came a really odd character, a middle-aged, man? woman? This person introduced themselves and provided sufficient and accurate information to make us happy they were indeed the resident and owner.

This person then for some reason said: *"I'll show you something interesting!"* and pointed to an outbuilding about half the size a single storey house which was partially covered in ivy and low branches from a nearby tree. We followed the person over to it and all the time they were saying *"this will give you an idea of what I do"* and *"this will be fun."* As we got to the only entrance-exit of the building, which also had no windows, I could see loads of high capacity thick cabling entering the building under the doorway. The door opened and the line of cables ran along a wooden floor made up of plywood boards into a single room, a few lights were on and it was very warm.

The person walked in first, again saying *"this will give you an idea of what I do"* followed by my colleague then I. As we crossed the threshold I leant forward and quietly said to the back of my colleague *"We're about to get arse raped!"* that made him laugh uncontrollably, the person was now looking at us, were they sizing us up or totally unaware we were freaked!

We followed the cables and entered the room, computer screens filled the walls all around, each with different images taken from satellites displayed on them and the person continually telling us this gives us an idea of what they did! This person was mad! We didn't stay long but did get sufficient information to pass on to the Hi-Tech Crime unit in case whatever the person was doing was shady!

It would be great to carry on telling stories that are light-hearted and where nobody is a victim, but sadly, however, the reality of the department I was in, is that on a daily basis we were all exposed to a relentless volume of major trauma incidents, it was not all funny quotes and interesting stops, but they helped mind you.

During my time within the Roads Policing Unit, and according to the reports of Suffolk County Council and the

Police & Crime Commissioner, there were over 1800 collisions where one or more occupants were killed or seriously injured, and there were over 9000 collisions where one or more occupants suffered minor injuries. A total of over 10,800 in Suffolk alone.

Add to this the number of attempted or actual bridge jumps, and you can see it's quite a number of this type of traumatic incident that we attended. I cannot find a report on the number of times Police attended for when someone suicidal was on the bridge, but not many weeks past without us attending to talk someone down.

Owing to this I was exposed to a very high volume of distress, pain and injuries of varying levels, but before I mention just a couple of the collisions, I want to take this opportunity to mention the great and amazing work I witnessed from the East Anglian Air Ambulance and, the ground NHS Ambulance crews.

At every serious collision I attended, they worked their utter socks off to help save lives and sadly it wasn't always enough. The East Anglian Air Ambulance (EAAA), which formed in the year 2000 is a charity that provides 2 helicopters crewed with specialist critical care pre-hospital Drs and critical care paramedics. They attend a vast range and high volume of major trauma emergencies for the counties of East Anglia, 365 days per year, delivering first-class critical care treatment to patients and then transporting them to an appropriate hospital. To date, they have completed well over 25,000 missions, and all of this is done without receiving any direct funding from the government.

It is financed purely through public donations, and what makes this even better for the residents of East Anglia is, that unlike a lot of other countries, if they fly out, perform lifesaving treatment on you and then fly you to a suitable hospital, you do not end up with an invoice dropping through your door demanding any money and possibly bankrupting you for their help.

It is truly a blessing that this can happen and something that with peoples support can continue.

I have seen the pilot land the helicopter in the road, on fields, in car parks and gaps a lot of motorists couldn't even park a car properly in! I have the utmost respect for them and in particular, the work I witnessed the critical care doctor (CCD), who was on the air ambulance perform. It was nothing shy of utterly miraculous and at times major league hard-core! A few examples of this, not to gore anyone out, but to make you appreciate the levels these people go to and the expertise used, to keep a loved one alive! And as an added bonus, for a while, His Royal Highness Prince William was the pilot for the Air Ambulance, touching down and showing an interest in the collisions he attended, always getting out to have a chat with emergency services (once things were calm, unless an immediate evacuation to the hospital was needed), and to think, little did the victims know that they were being taken by him to the hospital. The Royal family helping to care for its citizens is a lovely touch I think.

Fatal Collision – A young male had been ejected from a vehicle following a crash, he was not wearing his seatbelt. The usual CPR techniques and defibrillator had not been successful, and the male was going to die. As a last ditch effort to save his life, the CCD cut open the chaps chest, lifted the rib cage up for an Officer to hold and manually pumped the heart with his hand! I remember the Dr saying, *"he can't live without the heart pumping, but can live with broken ribs!"* Sadly the chap died despite this very advanced form of life support.

Serious Collison – A cyclist had been hit by a car and was deemed to have life-threatening injuries and needed fluids fast. The CCD took out what in essence looked like normal household battery powered drill, and then proceeded to drill holes into the shins and shoulders, through the flesh and into the bone so he could put a drip directly into the marrow of the bone, this person survived.

Serious Collison – A van driver crashed into a tree and brick wall, again suffered life-threatening injuries and had major internal bleeding. The CCD took out a knife, slit the drivers gut open and shoved his hand in, after a few moments he said: *"I've got the bleeding stopped."* I was watching over in disbelief and I remember saying to him, *"is this a bloody roadside autopsy?!"* The driver survived.

There are so many accounts of their great work I could make a book of those alone!

It was an absolute honour and great privilege to be around these people when working, a truly great sight that many only get by watching an edited TV show. I have helped them by holding body cavities open, doing CPR, inserting various tubes, supported organs and the greatest honour came from being able to help carry the stretcher and assist loading a patient into the helicopter, knowing the patient is receiving the highest quality care, and now being taken for further treatment by a modern miracle where lives matter more than money.

The National Health Service (NHS) ground ambulances and the fast response critical care cars of the Suffolk Accident Rescue Service (SARS) were staffed by fully qualified paramedics and critical care Dr's, who in the last few years of my service started to carry a new device which

I was lucky enough to witness a number of times; an automated chest compression device. If you've not seen one working, Google or YouTube it! It is utterly brutal, but is a bloody good depiction of just how much force you can use when doing CPR by hand! At the end of the day, the heart must beat, or you will die, simples.

Then there were the collisions where no matter how good the Dr or equipment, nothing could be done. After all, if someone is decapitated, had their head crushed flat or their body is blown to pieces what can they do! The forces involved in a collision are immense, even at low speeds and although the human body is an amazingly resilient thing, it is no match for solid bars impaling a head or chest, a fence post skewering vital organs, a truck wheel crushing someone's head and trees forcing engine components into the body as I have unfortunately witnessed over the years.

The following are brief accounts of just a few of the fatal collisions I attended, ones I remember for different reasons. I have purposely kept, dates, locations and gender out of them, out of respect for the families involved.

This is **not** an attempt at glorifying a fatal crash, but done as yet another way to help you realise the things I and other emergency service personnel had to deal with on a daily basis, and this coupled with everything else in this book, I hope is helping build the picture of why I am who I am, and why Police Officers can be a funny bunch of people.

A single vehicle collision occurred on a rural 60mph road involving a powerful car with a single occupant. The road had a good long straight and then a tight elevated right-handed bend, all lined with trees set back about 10 yards from the road. As I approached the scene I could see tyre marks through the grass starting at the outside edge of the bend, these tracks then continued running relatively parallel to the road through the grass, leading to the cars final resting place about 100 yards further up. It had embedded with such force head-on into the tree, (this tree's diameter was only about 10 inches), that it had dissected the car down the centre tearing it almost in half lengthways. The engine compartment and front cabin had become one and only the drivers disfigured head and forearm could be seen amongst the twisted, oily metal. The vehicles control panel which was now hanging out of the window opening of the front door, leaving the speedometer on show to the outside world, showed the needle had frozen at the 86mph position (a modern function of vehicles to assist in high velocity, sudden stop collision investigations).

Bearing in mind the distance the vehicle had been off the road, for it to still be at 86mph upon collision shows just how fast it must have been going as it entered the bend, before losing control.

Further up the road, and I mean some way up the road, a good couple of hundred yards, laid the front headlight cluster, this had become detached in the collision and continued on with the momentum of the vehicle like a missile. Now looking back towards the car it resembled a transformer wrapping itself around the tree. Death must have been quick! The fire crews cut away the twisted metal and engine block allowing us access to the driver, which we literally peeled out the cabin and laid on the floor. Once medical staff confirmed what we all knew, I then had to check the drivers' clothes for any identity documents, as I moved each limb they felt like cool, heavy jelly, not a solid bone was left in the body.

The next day, I drove the route of this collision and I entered the very same bend in my vehicle designed for rapid driving, and with me being used to and trained for high-speed driving. I hit the same bend, but at 60mph, and that felt very uncomfortable. If I had gone any faster, then a loss of control would have followed, it was a real show of just how much excess speed this person had been using for the bend. It was way too quick, or as is said in the Police, TFF (Too F**king Fast).

During the early hours of the morning, a call to a multi-lane road, where a car had gone into the back of a stationary 44-ton articulated goods vehicle, which had been parked in a layby at the edge of the road.

Upon arrival, there were no skid marks and no marks from the driver trying to correct an out of control vehicle, it was as though the vehicle had gone straight in, with absolutely no avoiding action being taken, the car had buried itself up to the boot peeling the roof back like a tin opener and squashing the car to half of its original size, the single occupant was very clearly dead. The force of the impact had caused the drivers head to erupt and explode, sending pieces of flesh, bone and brain all around the inside of the vehicle. It was not fun picking through this mess to find ID documents and search for any mobile phone.

Daytime in a residential street, a young child was out playing. Completely unaware of the child's presence, which was hidden by thick plant foliage, a vehicle entered the road and knocked down the child. The wheels went over the child's head, popping the eyes from the sockets and crushing the skull, large pools of thick blood had covered the child's face and the road surface around.

As I arrived, a parent was holding the child and understandably screaming in horror at what had happened and the current look of the child they loved. Despite the huge amounts of effort through CPR, and medical assistance the child was pronounced dead and taken to the hospital. With the scene closed off to the public, a constant thought in my head was the parents must not come back and see any trace of their child's blood, tissue or bone on the road, so I used bucket after bucket of soapy water, scrubbing away the signs of what had occurred. This collision was a real eye-opener owing to having kids of a similar age, and once everything had been sorted, the thoughts and images of my own child raced through my mind once again. It was a complete tragedy and one that must have been so horrific for the parents.
I send my love and best wishes their way.

During a night shift, a vehicle had broken down on one of the 70 mph multi-lane roads and had come to a stop, broadside across one of the lanes. With electrical power gone the vehicle was in complete darkness, the three occupants were clambering out the vehicle as a number of other vehicles approached completely unaware of the stranded vehicle. One of them impacted it fully, sending it spinning in the road, one occupant was killed outright by being crushed, another seriously injured whom later died and the third thrown by the force of the vehicle spinning like a bird across the road, and even across all of the opposing lanes before landing on the opposite embankment and thankfully did not suffer any major injuries and survived.

Dayshift again on a 70mph road, traffic had stopped for an incident further up the road, sat at the back of the queue was a vehicle with two children and an adult, a 44-ton goods vehicle was inbound for the queue, with the driver completely unaware of what was ahead. When the driver finally realised there was a stationary queue, it was too late, the goods vehicle then smacked into the back of the car crumpling it up like a squashed loaf of bread into the vehicle in front, all occupants died. You can make your own mind up as to why the driver didn't see this queue, but a modern electronic gadget will be a good starter!

A rural 60mph road, two motorcyclists were heading rapidly down a long bumpy straight, the lead bike hit a bump in the road too fast, causing it to veer across the road into the front of an oncoming vehicle, the rider then hitting the windscreen with such force it can only be described as like a bug hitting your own vehicle's windscreen and exploding. Even though full leather bike gear and helmet were worn, segments of flesh were sent flying into the bushes, the trees, the road and the field alongside and completely covered the second rider with a large volume of blood spray/mist before they could stop. Internal organs had been sent at speed along the road surface, partially cooking them from the heat of the friction. A truly horrific scene.

A rural country road, an elderly motorcyclist failed to make a left-handed bend and continued straight ahead, hitting a raised grass bank launching man and machine through the air, the rider was unfortunately wearing an open-faced helmet and face planted the corner of a brick built home, no matter how long I performed CPR I was unable to save this person's life, he suffered catastrophic head injuries.

Two people were out riding their own motorcycles, out enjoying a day's ride, travelling along the multi-lane road when a momentary action of another caused the front of the two riders to go down, the body slid along the road surface and hit the central barrier on its journey, the force of which made it act like a ham slice and completely decapitated the riders head, the second rider stopped in horror at what was going on. When we arrived my colleague was approached by the distraught rider who was saying, *"I can't find the head,"* that would later be found a few hundred yards up the road in the verge. In a blink of an eye things like this can happen, a surefire testament to why as road users we should all pay that little bit more attention and look out for each other.

A single lane country road, a group of friends were out in a car having spent the day together, as they drove along the driver's actions caused a loss of control of the car. The car impacted a number of trees as it spun down the road, and with it being fuelled by petrol it ignited following the collision. By the time Police, Fire and Ambulance arrived, the car and all within it had been burnt to death, leaving their charred skeletal remains unrecognisable from any photos and the smell lingering in the air and on our clothes for some time after. And to think, a Police Family liaison officer would have to explain this to the families of all involved.

One dark night shift, a person was walking along the side of a busy road, staggering about as if drunk. A 44-ton Artic approached from behind and as it went to pass the person, they staggered into the path of the vehicle leaving no time for any reaction. The vehicle struck the person sending them careering along the road surface causing massive burns to the front of their face and a caved in head from the rear. The person died at the scene.

I think you get the idea by now! These are only a few of the fatal collisions I attended, saw and dealt with.

From this point in an incident, three main things then happened, the investigation, involving; a collision reconstruction, statements, mechanical vehicle exams, drug/alcohol investigations and interviews. A trained Family Liaison officer would be assigned to the family of the deceased (I'll explain this later) and the dead bodies would be taken to the mortuary and placed in the fridge for the impending post mortem and family identification.

I always found it an odd feeling arriving at the mortuary, stripping the deceased of clothing, and sliding them on a metal tray into the floor to ceiling high fridges. When you opened the door, there was row upon row of shelves normally with naked bodies on each, some died in crashes, murders, old age you name it they had it, a very strange and thought-provoking sight that I would one day be laying in there like them!!!!

During my time within the Roads Policing Unit, I became trained as a family liaison officer, this was a role that exposed officers to a tremendous amount of stress and emotion. It was written in the manual of guidance that this must be a voluntary role for that very reason. Now, luckily for the Constabulary our entire Dept. had got trained for this role, we had all volunteered according to a senior officer, *"you can do this and stay on the Dept. or you can be moved to a different dept."* kind of volunteering!!! That went down very well with most of us.

To explain the family liaison officer (FLO) role, I think it best to take you on a journey showing what it involved, this is an actual case I became assigned to as the FLO, on this occasion I was paired with my colleague as he was newly trained and had to be with another officer.

Although it is much easier to cope with and also an official recommendation that FLO's always be paired, it was in fact, a rarity, mainly down to the lack of staffing following severe governmental funding cuts to British policing.

Our Dept. which did have roughly 40 officers dedicated to and specifically trained to Policing the roads, had to be cut to about 20 officers. It was sold to the public however that our dept. hadn't been cut, but had in fact grown. How???? Before the cuts, the Constabulary had a Firearms Dept. to deal with high-risk violent offenders and incidents where a firearm was known or believed to be involved and the Roads Policing Unit. When the cuts happened the two got merged together and the firearms officers were given the typical white cap of the RP officer and then sold to the public as extra RP officers. Anyway, I digress…

I arrived at work on a late shift starting at 2 pm and as soon as I walked through the door I was given my assignment, there had been a fatal motorcycle collision occur just moments before we arrived and officers were already on scene. We were to attend to look at the scene and then be briefed on our role as FLO's for this collision.

We gathered together the various bits of paperwork required for this role and headed out to the scene.

A motorcyclist had come off their bike and slid along the road surface into the path of an oncoming vehicle.

For our role as FLO, we looked at what was immediately obvious to have occurred, noted down identifying marks of vehicles and of the deceased rider, including the injuries sustained (they would be needed later), and after conducting various checks on the Police National Computer (PNC), we knew the name of the owner of the motorcycle - hopefully the deceased - the address it was registered to, and also how many occupants should be at the address, their names and their rough-ages. We discussed a number of factors and decided that on this occasion, I, would inform the occupants of what had occurred.

When we arrived at the address it was in a picturesque countryside setting. We found a vehicle in the driveway but we got no answer to the door, a check on PNC revealed this vehicle was registered to the spouse of the bike owner, so we knew we had the correct location.

We knocked on a couple of neighbours' doors trying to ascertain if anyone knew the whereabouts of the owners. Without any joy, we started to drive away from the location and we would return later. Whilst doing so, a vehicle passed us in the opposite direction, due to how remote the area was, we both thought that this could be the spouse. We turned and followed it and the vehicle did, in fact, turn into the long driveway and drove towards the house we had just been knocking at.

Knowing what I was going be doing very soon my stomach was somersaulting, the sentence I had formed was running through my mind over and over, the nerves rising and the feeling of destruction I am going to cause to someone's life with mere words running through my entire body.

I had done this many times before but each time the same, I am only human! I also had to be careful not to say anything that gives false hope or implies anything, for example, killed – someone could believe another person is at fault.

The vehicle stopped and the driver got out, with an innocent smile on their face the person jokily said *"sorry, was I speeding?"* at that very moment two young children got out of the vehicle also, bugger! This is not what I wanted.

I asked the driver to tell the kids to sit in the vehicle for a moment and with that, the persons face completely changed from a smiley happy character to a face of "what the hell?" After all, Roads Policing Officers don't make many pleasant house calls. With the kids away I said, *"Are you the spouse of…………..?"* Yes was the reply, *"Can I ask where …………….currently is?"* *"gone out on the motorbike for a bit, it was the person's birthday,"* was the response. Here we go then…*"There has been a collision involving the motorbike registered to…………. And as a result, the person I believe to be called……………..has died."* That was it, I had just stabbed the person in the heart with my words. With a staggering walk of disbelief and tears bursting from their disbelieving eyes the person collapsed to the ground a few steps from the front door.

My colleague took responsibility for the kids and luckily was very good with them. The shocked spouse who was trying to process my words gathered the strength to get up, unlock the door and enter the house. My colleague and the kids headed to a playroom out of the way, the person sat on the couch and I sat next to them and was asked: *"What did you say happened?"* *"A motorcycle registered to…………..has been involved in a collision, the rider who I believe to be…………… has died,"* I said.

The person sat quiet and motionless for a few seconds and then with no warning, flung their arms around me, holding me really tight and just cried out loud for about 15 minutes. I did my best to offer some comfort but knowing anything I say will at this moment not be heard, I just sat there and returned the hug.

Once the person had composed themselves a bit, I was told it was the rider's birthday and some family would soon be coming round, and right on cue, people started to arrive, I was asked to tell them what had happened too. Now that some family were there, my colleague and I left them for a while so we could make some arrangements and we would return later that evening.

We arranged for the identification process at the mortuary to done that evening and started to write our log of events.

When we later returned to the house there was only the spouse and one other relative present, we explained the requirement for someone to formally identify the body to us and that it had been arranged for in a few hours' time. I explained the condition of the body to the pair so they were under no illusions of what would lie ahead. The rider had suffered severe facial injuries and had also been torn from the groin up to the chest by the impact of the collision. This was information they found almost impossible to comprehend, after all, they had seen the rider only hours earlier alive and well.

We drove them to the mortuary and explained what was required of them and answered any questions the best we could. When we arrived, I sat the family in a quiet room whilst I went through to the chapel of rest, where the deceased was laid on a bed in a dedicated room with a red velvet blanket covering them and the ever-present light scent of lavender from the air system (covers the smells of the deceased).

The mortuary staff, knowing when families would be viewing a body, worked absolute marvels, with what was a bloody and torn body at the scene, they did their utmost to make the person easier to see for the family, and quite often it was not an easy task.

Once I had confirmed this was the same body from the collision, I asked the spouse and relative into the room to confirm to me it was, in fact, the person we believed.

Every single time I did this you could tell without saying a single thing, they walked in and as soon as they saw the person they loved, the person they had seen only hours previously, expecting them home again soon, the reality of the truth hit them like a hammer. I always gave them some time alone with the deceased whilst I completed the next bit of paperwork.

After that, we drove them home, answered any questions they had and arranged to see them again in the morning. Over the coming months, we would become regular visitors, delivering investigation updates, returning property, answering questions, offering support and going through the entire investigation paperwork and post mortem results with them, readying them for the inquest into the person's death that would follow when the collision investigation was complete. We were the families point of contact in relation to this collision.

In this particular case we became very friendly, they were an incredibly nice and genuine family. It made my role easier and less impactive on me personally, but one of the problems this role causes, is due to the continual exposure to an environment of grief, although not one of your loved ones, you see and are with grief regularly, and it does affect you. Seeing the kids of similar age to my own and how they were dealing with the loss of a parent was very saddening and hit home hard with me. These kids were the same age as mine and it was impossible not to think about how mine would be if it was I that had died.

Once the inquest has been and gone we would gently slip out of the lives of the family allowing them to try and achieve some kind of normality. After the months of being with them, people would sometimes find it hard not to have the officer with them, they saw them as a pillar of support and a link to the final moments of their loved ones, a moment they did not see themselves. I ended this FLO deployment with a really nice photo of me and the family (at their request), and I still have it today and hope by me being there I helped, even just a little bit, especially for those utterly adorable kids.

Remembering the few fatal collision examples I gave you a moment ago, you can see this was not an easy task being a FLO, and one that caused great emotional strain.

Whilst I believe this was a vital and very much needed role, it was one I found very draining both emotionally and physically, we would be performing tasks for this role whilst still doing our day to day work and dealing with all the other incidents as normal. It was common for a FLO to feel stretched and stressed out, and sadly the role was downplayed by a few of the firearms officers, all of which did not have to perform this vital role and saw it as nothing more than an 'agony message' (notifying a family of a death). This would be the single most common cause for debate amongst some officers within the dept.

Being a FLO also exposed you to people when grief can be expressed in varying ways.

I was deployed as FLO, alone, to a family following another fatal collision. As I drove to their address which was over an hour from my base I remember hearing a particular song played on the radio, it was repeated a few times during my journey and is now one that I cannot listen to without recalling this FLO deployment, it is Avicii's 'Wake Me Up'. During my time on the Roads Policing Unit, a number of other songs would trigger memories of horrific incidents and things I had dealt with, to me the phrase - the magic and also the misery of music! Is very true.

When I arrived, I found they lived in a block of flats, in an area known for high crime and unsavoury people. I sat before a group of 9 people in their living room explaining what had happened to their deceased family member. Each of them hated the Police and were not afraid of saying so, even under these tragic circumstances!

I was told how they would happily firebomb police stations and fight any officer who tried to exert any authority over them. *"What am I doing here?"* I thought. The feeling of vulnerability, unfortunately, must have made me perform my role very differently.

Whenever I called them, I would be shouted at for minutes on end down the phone, I could have just hung up, but a family member of theirs had just died, I kept thinking. Then, when going over the investigation paperwork with them, they did not agree that their relative was to blame for their own death, and they'd had their views corroborated by a fortune teller, so they erupted - shouting, yelling, banging things, saying the Police have fixed the findings due to who they were and called me an out and out liar! That was it and I told them so, fucking idiots! I would not be seeing or speaking to them again, and they can wait for any other findings at the inquest and won't have me to go through anything else or help them with a single thing. I'm done.

A few experiences like that and the ever increasing pressure on me due to increased short staffing and increasing demand started to make me hate certain aspects of the job, not the organisation, I loved them and still do. I had started to change mentally. Every day before work or last thing before I went to bed I would find myself checking the news for any fatality, hoping none had occurred before I got to work and would have to perform the role of FLO as soon as I walked in the door.

Weekends would see the worst time for my mind, during spring, summer and autumn the number of fatalities climbed dramatically, partly due to the increasing number of motorcycles on the road. Not many summer weekends passed without a fatality or very serious collision.

After years of seeing countless families change following a death or people being unable to walk, talk and speak again after serious collisions, I did get very frustrated and also angry with those people who had been in a minor collision, where hardly even a light cluster was cracked and the occupants would be rolling around in what looked like absolute agony, the money signs in their eyes and thinking of getting as much compensation as they could. Instead of Whip-lash, we used to call it "Whip-cash."

If ever I had reason to believe the pain was exaggerated or fake, be it by a paramedic telling me they were fine, the very low level of collision they were in or because of the type of vehicle they were in, I was sure to tell them what I thought and would be sure to document my views on the collision record, so that any pursuing lawyer who applied for a copy of the record saw exactly what medical staff and the officer attending the scene thought and saw. It was these people that made insurance premiums skyrocket for the other motorists. After years of this environment, I could tell when someone had an honest injury, and in that case, I did everything I could to help.

To cheer things up a bit I shall tell you of a few of my own close shaves.... and a crash I was involved in.

It is an inevitable truth that Police officers driving at high speeds, on very busy roads, in higher risk environments and performing higher miles daily than most civilian drivers, is that they will be at an increased risk of collision.

In my opinion, the British Police, and in particular the Roads Policing Unit, are amongst the highest trained Police drivers worldwide. To be in the Dept. they have completed 8-10 weeks of 5 days a week, 9 hours a day driver training just to sit in the driver's seat of the high-performance Roads Policing cars, and then being refreshed for another 2 weeks every few years after that, nobody could say otherwise. Some countries would give their Police all of the law training, safety training, scenarios and driver training in that time, not just dedicated driver training!

All of them, however, are only human, even the highest trained, full time, professional race driver's crash. I mean, the public crash dawdling along at 30mph just on their way to the shops without a care in the world for heaven's sake!

I was driving at 120 mph along the A12, I was in the overtaking lane, gaining on a large goods vehicle, restricted to 56mph, I could see there were no obstructions, or other vehicles ahead of it. As I was about to commit to passing the vehicle, it swerved violently into my path and back out again, forcing me to anchor on hard, making the nose of my car almost peel the tarmac off the road surface, my vehicle stepped into the beginnings of a sideways slide, luckily I managed to control it and avoided a serious collision. I'm sure many of you have witnessed these large vehicles do a huge swerve almost as though done just to keep other drivers on their toes!

Driving with blue lights and siren on one dayshift through one of Ipswich town centres one way systems by the docks, there were two lanes for the same direction of traffic. I was attending a collision and was making my way through the traffic and as normal with no dramas, then I began to pass a dark car with a doddery old lady at the helm. With my sirens still blaring and lights all flashing as I drew alongside her, she for no apparent reason stuffed her car into my lane and in turn ramming me towards a wall! I couldn't believe it!!

Well, after I had given out a few choice words about, keeping death off the roads and alike, she stated she saw me and had panicked, and didn't know what to do. *"Well stuffing it into my car wasn't the bloody answer, was it!"* To top off this lovely moment, she then declared to the world, I was *"hossing"* along, dangerously too fast. What she didn't realise is Police vehicles not only have video/audio recording, but they also have a data recorder, it showed I was passing her at 33mph! In a 30mph zone, hardly *"hossing"* I think you will agree.

Another trip down the A12, I was doing 135 mph when my rear tyre blew, this caused my vehicle to have an almighty weave around, again once controlled there were no issues, but it was damn exciting at the time!

Then there were times that the training you had in high speed, close proximity driving would come in very handy, even for the odd joke on a colleague.

One I particularly liked was this; I was at my base when a call came in requiring my immediate attendance.

A few moments prior to this, a colleague and friend from a different department had left my base to head back to his own station, completely unaware I was now attending an incident (as our Dept. had our own private talk group for incidents). I was heading down the 70mph road, the A12, and saw him ahead meandering along. I knew what had to be done! He was in the left lane driving steady and controlled along a straight section and I was in the overtaking lane, I was steady at 140 mph, as I drew closer I lined up to pass him leaving about a foot between our vehicles and BBOOOOMMMM! I passed him like a missile. The turbulence of my vehicle rocking his like a boat on the ocean, I then received a call to my vehicle's radio, it was him, laughing he shouted *"YOU BASTARD! YOU NEARLY BLEW ME OFF THE FUCKING ROAD!!"* extremely pleased with myself and laughing out loud, I could only muster *"you're welcome."*

Owing to what we witness and deal with, Police Officers can sometimes be misunderstood, they often have a dark sense of humour and seem to find things funny that most people think inappropriate. This is not in any way out of disrespect for someone or a situation, but more often than not a coping mechanism for dealing with the horrific things they have been involved in.

They can seem blunt, rude, cold-hearted and speak straight to the point, years of having to deal with arses who are drunk, someone who has raped a child or a drunk driver that has killed a family on the road, it can do that to you.

They get used to having to tell people in no uncertain terms what has happened, what is required of them, and order it to happen then and there. Despite this and the demands on them, they can still act with love and care, and often great restraint.

Take this example I dealt with, could you stay calm? Hold your tongue? And be professional? I was on supervision duty of a man who had been arrested for an unprovoked attack and raping of his 20 something-year-old daughter who was also heavily pregnant.

Sat in his cell, with me at the door, he was regaling me with his story as though he had achieved a god-like status through his actions. This went on for nearly an hour, how well he had done, she had deserved it, it doesn't matter, this is a waste of everyone's time, get me a drink, I want food, you have to do what I say. It continued on like that the whole time.

One prize remark he made, remembering it was his daughter, and that she was pregnant was; *"you know the best thing? It was like getting rough sex from the bitch and a blowjob from the baby all at the same time!"* It's things like that and people like that, which made me think I could sort society out if I could just shoot him in the face and have done with him, save the planet, the people and the oxygen from being wasted by him.

Once again Police uniform was to undergo another overhaul, we were now issued with black wicking shirts, black fleece sweaters, black combat trousers and improved body armour.

As is always the case, A few complaints were made from the public that the Police now looked more paramilitary than needed. But from a practitioners point, the uniform was comfortable and practical, all going towards helping get our job done easier. The only complaint I had was wearing all black in the summer was not fun!

With the new uniform came my next new Roads Policing car, this time with a diesel engine! A Police Spec BMW 530d M Sport. With the huge advancements in power and efficiency of modern diesel engines this vehicle would now knock the Volvo T6 into touch, it had a 260 horsepower Bi-Turbo engine, with a few modifications. An 8-speed Tiptronic gearbox with paddle shift gearing by the steering wheel, it was rear wheel drive with 413lb per ft. torque and hurtled from 0-62mph in 5.8 seconds, also limited to 155mph[8], it was a beast! And fast became my favourite police vehicle, so much so that one of the driving instructors on a refresher course with me said: *"this car is like an extension of your foot."* I loved it!

© Jeremy H Cohen. We now referred to them by the last 3 characters of the index plate. This car was NNR. Taken on Portal Avenue, Martlesham.

© Jeremy H Cohen. NNR at the scene of a collision on Bramford Rd at the Junction with Yarmouth Rd, Ipswich.

© Jeremy H Cohen. The sister car to mine, this one is NNT. I would make the news driving this vehicle, a story told later in this book. Image taken on the A12 Southbound at Martlesham.

My new car, NNR, would sadly be my chariot in a collision that would see it needing a full transmission change, oil sump change, new wheel and new bumper, a lot of expensive damage.

It was about 2 am and I was on a night shift attending an emergency incident about 15-20 miles away. I was travelling along the A14 at about 120mph. The road was quiet and dry. As I passed junction 54 heading eastbound at the village of Sproughton, I got the quickest flash of something on the road, lit for a minuscule of a second by my headlights, there was absolutely nothing I could do, and any last minute swerve would have resulted in me doing a barrel roll.

I went over this item and it launched my car into the air, crashing me back down with a horrible thud. I could tell immediately the car was very ill, it had only minimal power and made some horrible sounds. I limped it the next safe spot and informed another officer to go and collect whatever the item was to prevent another collision.

To my surprise, as I slowly climbed the hill towards Copdock, I saw 2 other cars stopped with their emergency hazard lights flashing, I drew in behind them and they stated they had both hit the same object, disabling their vehicles also. Within a few moments, a fuel tanker then came crawling up to us, it too had hit the object, causing damage. This time though the object was now lodged under the tanker, and to my disbelief, it was a twisted up section of central barrier! The stuff designed to be strong enough to deflect cars off in a crash.

When I watched back my cars' video, I did, however, have to laugh at a few choice words that came out of my mouth when I was sent airborne, but I doubt my friends in the Police vehicle workshops would have laughed knowing the task that now laid ahead of them!

Whilst on the subject of choice words!! As any Police officer or Police incident dispatcher will tell you, sometimes things said on the radio can make you laugh or cry, whether it be the horror of what is happening or something someone has said without realising the words coming out of their mouth, two moments of mine were as follows.

Owing to our Dept. covering the entire county, which was split into several radio talk group areas, for a while, we for some reason had to announce to the dispatcher of the various areas as we entered their talk group area. Well, without thinking, this one time I called up *"VL from RC91,"*

VL is the call sign for our control room and RC91 was my specific call sign for that day, each call sign gave the dispatchers information to assist them in finding the most suitable units for incidents. This call sign as an example showed; R – Roads Policing, C – Car, 9 – based at HQ and 1 – The intended patrol route (although we would be sent anywhere required within the county and quite often beyond, into Essex, Cambridgeshire, and Norfolk).

The lady dispatching for this area said, as is normal "*Go ahead RC91*" I then declared to the entire talk group "*Thank you, I have just come in your patch*" a moments silence followed and then with the sound of her holding back laughter she calmly replied, "*received.*" It took me a moment to realise what I had said and I was sure not to make that mistake again!

The second time, was after I had been dispatched to move a dead badger from the overtaking lane of the A14. When I arrived there was also a couple of other animals dead on the road, which I also moved. With a moment's quick wit I thought of a suitable update to my status, "*VL from RC96*" (note a different patrol route), "*Go ahead RC96*" "*I have arrived and seem to have come across a Wind in the Willows suicide pact.*" I personally found this funny but I don't think the dispatcher understood my sense of humour, never mind!

It was a regular task moving dead animals from the fast roads, all to stop some inattentive driver swerving last minute to avoid it and crashing into someone, it did, however, give me the opportunity for a different kind of humour. I found great fun in chasing my colleagues with dead animals, particularly deer. Don't know why but I thought it was funny, as they'd run off shouting "*Jerry!*"

Suffolk Constabulary's Roads Policing Unit took pride in providing its officers with the training needed to perform the many roles officers had to perform, whilst within the Roads Policing unit I received the following training on top of any courses I'd already received based at Ipswich and Hadleigh these were;

Police Advanced Driving – You know about this one already.

Police Pursuit Commanders course – Again, you know this one.

Traffic Patrol Officers law course – This was a course designed only for RP officers, it was a 3-week intensive course covering the various road traffic rules and regulations, this was a very in-depth course and successful completion gained me an external qualification issued by the Institute of the Motor Industry.

Family Liaison Officers certification – This was a 1-week course, I have told you a bit about this one too.

Field Impairment Test and Drug recognition certification – This was the one you see on TV when a drunk or druggy is made to walk on a line, touch their nose, raise a foot etc.… It was good fun watching people fumble about trying to complete the tasks when high on some drug. I remember one chap was instructed to stand still, and raise one foot 6 inches off the ground with his leg extended out to the front. I always demonstrated what was required before each test as words can be confusing to some. Well, this chap obviously had no idea what I was on about and he took up a stance resembling the crane that the Karate Kid and Mr Miyagi would have been proud of. Bloody idiot. He got arrested.

Police vehicle examiners course - this was a 3-week intensive course used to enable officers to perform a more advanced mechanical examination of vehicles at the roadside and also following a collision to prove/disprove a defect as being a contributory factor in a collision. This was done as a matter of course for fatal collisions, life-altering collisions and when a driver, in their defence, stated a defect had caused the collision.

The qualified officer would gain a nationally recognised qualification and be able to present the evidence obtained as a matter fact to the courts. When trained in this discipline the officer also had the authority to examine a vehicle at the roadside and then subsequently immediately prohibit it from use on a road due to a defect found that posed a risk to any other person, be it a motorist, a pedestrian, the occupants and the driver. It was not even allowed to be towed, it had to be lifted totally off the road. I shall cover a vehicle exam in a bit…

Analogue and Digital Tachograph analysis - This was a 3 week intensive course that gained you another external qualification with the Institute of the Motor Industry, it enabled you to examine, decipher and prosecute for drivers hours infringements of the Heavy goods vehicles, and to examine the physical data recorders to look for evidence of fraudulent use or tampering.

Goods vehicle weight examination - This was an internal course that enabled you to require a goods vehicle, large or small to go with you to a weigh station to check for any infringements with regards to its weight. I remember I stopped one goods vehicle for a weight check and at the roadside I wanted the back to be opened up so I could see what the load was. When the doors opened it was packed floor to ceiling with various household and garden items, absolutely jam-packed, but right by the door, there was also a small freestanding kitchen stall, upon which a lady was sat facing me with a look of utter surprise on her face. The driver received a ticket and the lady was made to walk.

Taser training - I was trained in the use of the X26 Taser. These were being rolled out to a large number of officers, much to the dislike of the public! Remember me saying British policing was borne on the idea that the police were empowered by the people, not by the force of the state? You now see why it's so hard for the British police to be armed, the public hated Tasers which were next to useless unless the person was wearing summer clothing and if it was really windy then no chance! So guns were easily out of the question. Although recent terrorist attacks in the UK have opened the debate up again.

There were the basics that we all got like, roadside drug testing, roadside alcohol testing, handheld and in-car speed detection equipment and ANPR (Automatic Number Plate Recognition) systems, again I'll mention this in a bit and the fast roads safety course – Also one I've already touched on.

So, what is ANPR? Automatic Number Plate Recognition, this is an absolute asset to modern policing and one I believe every single police officer should have access to. ANPR is a nationwide database full of all the car registration numbers, whenever a car or number plate are stolen, it is updated onto this database, when vehicles are uninsured, untaxed, linked to people with no driving license, drink drivers, people with intelligence reports against them, been used in the course of crime, been used by drug runners etc. etc., they are also updated on to the database, and a marker is added to the registration plate.

All Roads Policing vehicles and some of the local patrol vehicles have cameras fitted in them that are linked to a computer within the car, the computer receives updates daily and sometimes more often, with any newly added data. There are also cameras fitted to road signs, bridges, posts etc. around the entire country, for the best part in discreet locations.

When vehicles pass the in-car or static camera, the registration plate of that car is automatically read and checked on the database, if there is a marker on that plate, then almost instantly, a second or two, it is brought to the attention of whoever is monitoring that camera, so the in-car camera, the driver will see and hear a notification on the in-car computer screen, and any police dispatchers monitoring the fixed cameras will see any markers on their screen. The marker will have a very quick reference to see, for example, STOLEN, TAX, MIDAS (Insurance) DRUGS etc. to enable a quicker response to intercept that vehicle, more detailed information is also available if needed at the touch of a button.

With this system there is the ability to show patterns of travel, vehicles always travelling together and a search function to see if particular vehicles have activated anywhere in the country. I'm sure you will agree that this sounds an incredible asset to the Police's job of preventing and dealing with offences.

A good example of this is, there have been a number of burglaries at the other end of the country, a registration plate has been witnessed, and a marker can then be added to that registration number "Seen in Sus Circs," that registration number then goes through a camera of an officer that had no idea this vehicle had even been doing anything wrong 100's of miles away and can then be stopped, details of occupants can be obtained, and a check on the identity of the vehicle can be made, to ensure there isn't a cloned plate. If grounds exist or any further info is available, then searches or arrests can be made.

Another example, you see someone drinking heavily in a bar and then get into a vehicle, you note the plate number and contact police, this can be immediately added to the database, then, as well as officers searching for the vehicle if it goes through a camera someone will know its location, if it's a car camera it can be stopped immediately, the officer may not see the plate for some reason but the camera, which also has infra-red night reading will. A drunk driver can be stopped and detained, and we all want those arseholes off the road I'm sure! I know I do.

One final example, a collision has occurred and one of the vehicles has fled the scene. If any details were noted by the other parties (colour, make, part of the index number or the whole index then a search can be made for like vehicles in that area at that time, enabling an Officer to investigate those vehicles for signs of damage/involvement at their registered addresses.

In a very brief and basic summary, that is ANPR. A brilliant tool and one used daily by our dept. with great success.

Now you have an idea of the skill sets available and have heard a few of the more serious incidents, how about I go through an average day of the RP officer, this does vary a lot dependant on the shift you work, days, lates and nights but I'll do a bog-standard everyday day shift for you.

Starting at 7 am, the team would be in, kitted up, vehicles ready, and hot tea in hand for 7 am prompt. We would then have a briefing with the supervisor and be told of any incidents/vehicles of note from the last shift, receive any new intelligence packages and be assigned our patrol area.

Following briefing, we would check for any new emails, and get our days to do list all ready, this is all assuming a job doesn't come in immediately, which it often did! Sometimes it was in the door and back out again before you've said hello to anyone.

We would then go out and for the first few hours it was the rush hours, we dealt with any crashes that had occurred, assist with some broken vehicles, move some debris and then the roads would calm down a bit. Now was the time we could focus on any statements we needed to take for crashes or other cases we are investigating or if we're up to date, a chance for some proactive time.

I'd spend some of the time parking in various hidden spots looking for people not wearing their seatbelts or using their phones, and have the ANPR camera set to read all the cars that passed where I was. I'd typically issue a few tickets, maybe seize a car for no insurance and then before you knew it, it was lunchtime.

Lunch, if you were having a quieter day was a nice break and time to catch up with your team, on other days you never got the chance to have it, or you'd start it and then have to go out, leaving your food to waste.

After lunch, I would concentrate on stopping older looking vehicles, conducting roadside mechanical exams and issuing tickets for any identified offences, and if severe prohibit the vehicle from use.

Occasionally, I would take a vehicle to the weighbridge if I found the time, but that was quite laborious and I didn't do it that often

During the afternoon, just like the morning, you would be continually required to attend the big roads for debris, collisions, and more broken down vehicles…

Towing vehicles would often bring its own entertainment, with members of the public never having been towed before and sometimes with a language barrier mixed in, there was usually something to laugh about.

I remember this one time that a taxi had broken down on the A14 about half a mile from the next junction off. I arrived first and a colleague was also on his way.

As is the norm, I got the towing eye and rope all set up on the front of the taxi and then briefed the driver on what will happen. *"My colleague will draw up in front of you and I will attach the tow rope to the rear of his car. I want you to turn your ignition key to unlock the steering, select neutral, apply the foot brake and release the parking brake. When you start to feel him pulling on your car, slowly release the brake so that you roll, but keeping the brake very slightly applied to prevent you from gaining speed down the slight hill. He will take you no more than 25mph and then off at the next junction into that truck stop. Any problems sound your horn and apply the brake to stop him. You must steer and you must brake. Understand?"* Well, the Indian taxi driver looked at me with either a vacant expression not understanding a word I was saying or it was an expression of *"I know what I'm doing Officer!"* We shall see…

My colleague arrived and I attached the rope and then made my way to my vehicle to follow with my rear fend off lights illuminated to warn other approaching motorists.

They started to move off and it was all going well until I saw from my view beneath the car that the rope was getting very slack between the two cars. I called my colleagues car set and spoke with him *"he's going to ram you!"* I said, *"maybe, we'll see!"* was the response. They approached the junction and started to move over to the exit lane. Coming up soon was a tight left-handed bend with a large chevron sign pointing traffic to the left, and a raised grass bank immediately in front of it.

I watched as the rope kept tightening and loosening as my colleague tried desperately to gain some tension between the two cars. As he slowed for the bend I saw the rope go extremely slack again, now hanging to the floor. My colleague made the tight left turn, and the Indian taxi driver didn't, instead, it kept going straight ahead, on a collision course with the chevron sign. As he started up the embankment the rope had tightened due to the angle my colleague was still going forward at, it tugged hard on the taxi, acting as a powerful bungee yanking the taxi harshly back in line with the road again, and then shooting it at a greater pace into the back of my colleagues car with an almighty crashing sound. My colleague stopped and got out, clearly pissed off and all red-faced, he slammed his door and shouting *"What the hell do you think you were doing!"* towards to the Indian chap as he walked over to him. I was in absolute floods of tears, it was brilliant and bloody hilarious. Still makes me die to this day.

Unfortunately for that same colleague, he would fall foul of my humour again, this time a few years on…

We were at a collision on the A12, everything had been sorted out and we were tidying the road in preparation for opening it to the public.

One of the cars involved had been severely impacted at the front corner, the wheel was buggered and the engine bay was all crumpled up. We had decided to hook up one of our cars and pull it to the edge of the road to free up one lane for the public.

With my colleague who was quite tall, struggling to clamber into the squashed up and damaged small car, I hooked it up to the ARV. The ARV crew told me to let them know when he was ready, well, he was nowhere near fully in yet and I couldn't resist! *"OK, he's ready!"* I shouted.

Owing to the damaged car being all crumpled up it required a good deal of force and a strong tug to move it, the ARV then pulled hard and suddenly, throwing my colleague back into the seat, he was now shouting to the ARV *"STOP! I'm not ready!"* The ARV crew couldn't hear him properly so I naturally helped with communication, *"He said, you need to really go for it!"* The ARV kept tugging really hard and abruptly jerking the car along whilst my colleague was shouting and cursing for them stop as he was being thrown about! He was livid! He was being thrown about and not listened to, thinking the ARV crew were trying to be funny. And I once again was reduced to a tearful wreck of laughter. Utter brilliance on my part!

Then sometimes the tables were turned on to me! My colleague Andy and I were double crewed on a night shift, we went to help a broken down car full of non-English speaking Romanians! It was dark, cold and damp. We decided I would steer the broken down car and Andy would pull us.

I sat in the driver's seat and had everything ready as normal. We were about 2 miles from the next off junction so it wouldn't take too long.
To complicate matters, the battery had died so there were no lights, no wiper blades and no fan to blow off the steamed up windscreen.

I let Andy know that this would be a trickier one and off we went, sat about 6ft from the back of the police car, my speed kept increasing, 20mph, 30mph, 40mph, 50mph…*"What on earth is he doing? He knows I can hardly see!!!"* We were cruising along, and then I remembered there was going to be a small tight roundabout with a sharp right turn we would have to negotiate on the exit.

As we drew closer to it, I was trying hard to slow us down with the brake, but with no power to the car, the brakes did not have the assistance of the servo, so I had to push harder than usual to slow down and they were therefore much less effective. The Romanians were all shouting *"Whoa! Whoa! Whoa!"* Obviously afraid of what was going on, I could barely see a thing through the fogged up glass, just the brake lights ahead.

Andy turned to the right and went around the roundabout barely losing any speed, with me desperately trying to follow and then also stop at the end, it was a hairy moment. When we had stopped I got out and saw Andy was in tears of laughter, obviously an intentional joke with me being the victim this time!

…With the day the drawing to an end, I'd do a quick tachograph check of a goods vehicle and then it would be back to base to plug the car into a huge data recorder where the ANPR would be downloaded and updated, wash and fuel the car and finish writing up any reports or tickets you had.

This example was when we had sufficient staff to share out incidents and also be proactive a vast majority of the time, this would change drastically, especially for me in the near future.

© Andrew Masterson. This is me, A14 Eastbound just prior to Junction 55 at Copdock. The two pins on my body armour are from the "Black Rat" collection, one a PG9 (prohibition) black rat and the other the generic symbol for the Black Rat.

The "Black Rat" was a term denoting the Traffic Police or Roads Policing Unit, as it is now more commonly known as. It is not seen as an insult and is a term that came about as historically the traffic officers would happily deal with their other non-traffic officer colleagues for offences, just like a black rat eating its own young. Some people also say it's because we got down and dirty, covered in vehicle dirt and grease or bodily fluids and grime from the horrific things we attended.

Some RP Officers used to put a Black Rat car sticker in their vehicles, in the hope that it would be seen if being stopped by another RP officer. In time, some criminals caught on to this and adopted the tactic, so it now actually increases your chances of being stopped, and as far as I know, not a practise done by officers for some time.

There is even an official website for "Black Rat" merchandise and any sales of the official black rat products go towards a fund for orphaned children of RP officers who are killed on duty.

With the upcoming changes on the horizon, one winter gave us a great opportunity for some RPU / Firearms bonding. The two teams with the highest trained drivers, and this often resulted in a quite competitive environment and banter between the two.

The RPU officers building was opposite the firearms building at the HQ, with a 10-metre concrete area between them. During this one evening, we had a really good snowfall and men being men, we couldn't resist the opportunity for a Snowball fight during our refs break, RPU vs Firearms. A clash of the titans!

It was brilliant! We used the external windows and doors as sites to launch attacks and seek cover, and dragon lights to blind the "enemy" allowing a barrage of snowballs to be launched their way, it was going well, and we were winning. Then, the firearms team formulated a new plan, they retreated for a brief moment into their building before emerging with full-length riot shields, approaching in close formation peppering us the whole way. We were being overrun, forcing us to seek shelter indoors, leaving the victors chanting and cheering outside, parading up and down now wearing our white hats taken from our vehicles. Ironically, little did they know that the changes coming our way would see them wearing them a lot more often, and not by choice!

My department had severe changes to adopt. We went from having four or five dedicated RP officers and one sergeant per shift, to two dedicated officers per shift and a couple of sergeants covering all of the shifts, plus one of the three bases was to be closed down, the Halesworth base was cut.

All of this was mainly down to the deep-reaching government funding cuts to British Policing, resulting in the Constabulary having to find money and move resources around as a direct result. We were an expensive dept, with high-performance vehicles, lots of training and expensive kit, it was inevitable we would be culled to some degree, and from then on, even with the skills available and expertise brought to the serious incidents we attended and dealt with, it was a constant battle to justify our existence and expense.

The firearms dept. then joined with us and it was sold as no change or even an increase of staff in the RP department, as there were now 5 or 6 officers per shift. There would be the two dedicated RPU officers, the double crewed ARV and a spare firearms officer (some shifts had two spare firearms officers), we would also now become a joint unit with the neighbouring force, Norfolk and were re-branded as the Roads Policing & Firearms Operations Unit (RPFOU), doesn't sound too bad does it…?

During the day to day life of Suffolk, the ARV & spare firearms officer(s), were more often than not deployed to firearms-related incidents and the local patrol areas also stole them to help backfill their dropping numbers, again due to the funding cuts. On top of this, the firearms officers received an incredible amount of training (quite rightly so), often taking the spare officers out of patrol for weeks on end. There would always be an ARV at each base working but as I've already said, they got eaten up daily. That would leave just me and my colleague to deal with the busiest area of the county for traffic-related incidents, and the majority of immediate response incidents received in the Constabulary.

For the next couple of years it wasn't too bad, and we coped, our days had started to change but we managed. We would be going from incident to incident non-stop for the entire shift a lot more often, but still found some days to do proactive work in any downtime, but not anywhere near to the extent we had been doing so previously.

What was really nice, is the majority of firearms officers also saw this and a couple, in particular, would often raise the point to the senior command that whenever they got deployed, we were left understaffed for the number of incoming incidents, which in turn left us vulnerable in a very dangerous environment.

Late shifts weren't as bad as days, once the rush hours had finished we had a decent amount of time to be proactive and my colleague and I would often do a late night speed check, on foot. We would park up somewhere and stop any and all cars with lights out and any over the speed limit, this was not to prosecute people at 5-10 mph over the limit, but it gave us a chance at having a high volume number of vehicles to check for drink/drug drivers, unsafe vehicles, people who were wanted etc. We did ticket some for speed but only when speeds were quite high mind you.

I actually used to enjoy it, especially on a cold evening, we would have our thermos mugs of hot tea and have a really good chat whilst working, but as is the nature of the beast, it was never long before we would be called away for incidents on the big roads.

Owing to the increased high daily mileage and wear from pursuits my car was to be replaced, staying with the same make/model and Police spec BMW, but a different colour and newer.

© Jeremy H Cohen. My newest pride and joy, CZB. I cannot remember where I took this one!

After getting used to working with just the 2 of us, it would always seem like a new place when the firearms officers had finished their latest round of training as we would get an extra person back to help us out, still not like the days of 5 dedicated RPU officers but an extra pair of hands nonetheless, the spare firearms officers were tasked with traffic patrol and to assist us with incidents, whilst they didn't have the experience or training for the role we did, it was a great relief. It also gave us a chance to mix things up a bit.

My colleague and I would alternate between another love of the job for us, for him, it would be taking out the Police motorbike if he fancied it, and I would take out an unmarked Roads Policing car. I loved my days in that! It was a day to be really proactive and it was quick too! So much fun could be had in it!!

A BMW 330 X-drive, like my normal patrol BMW, it had 8 gear paddle shift gearing, all the in-car kit, but was smaller and lighter. With the addition of the X-drive system giving the capability for all-wheel drive, it meant greater traction and handling in the bends. It had the same 3-litre Bi-Turbo engine as my other car but this hurtled from 0-62mph in 5.4 seconds and again was limited to 155mph[9]. It felt like an atom bomb, or as my old tutor called RP Cars, *"A Wolf in Sheep's clothing."*

On days with this, I spent more time in the towns, searching out offences that were harder to get when in a huge marked RPU car, phones, seatbelts, careless, dangerous and antisocial driving happened right in front of you, people didn't know any better until I lit up the blue lights, and it had lots, it was like a space ship when you turned them all on. In the grill, in the side mirrors, in the headlights (which alternate flash also), across the top of the windscreen, attached to the front bumper, built into the index plate, it was like a mass of blue.

I remember a few incidents in particular in which I loved using this car.
The first being simple but great, I was following a small car out of town and along a twisty country road, it had a huge rear window and I could see really clearly into the car. A

single male occupant was at the helm. As we negotiated the bends I noticed he started to become a touch jerky with his steering, he was fiddling with something. I then saw him raise his left hand to his left ear, with a mobile phone very clearly in his hand. Owing to the offence I lit my car up and put the siren on, indicating for him to stop, he visibly jumped in his seat and with the panic of an impending, £200 / $300 fine and 6 points on his driver's license he smashed his car in to the grass verge and subsequently the ditch alongside. It killed me, I found it bloody hilarious and took great pride in introducing myself to him.

The next, I was asked to attend a possible fatality, and when the location was added to my Satnav it was apparently 1 hour 30 minutes away! Well I stuck my emergency equipment on and went for it, most of the way it was single carriageway, 2 lanes of opposing traffic, with a mix of residential and rural areas, I was going tooth and nail and got there in considerably less time than predicted, something like 40 minutes of hard, full on driving, overtaking everything whilst also accounting for those that are out to kill you!

As I drew up in the street of the crash, I was exhausted and knew I'd now have to deal with this serious collision.

I stopped and was unbuckling my belt when a local patrol officer came over and started to open my door, relieved I was there and also nervous about being at the incident without Roads Policing. He started to speed talk at me, telling me about what had happened and what he had done so far. *"Hang on a second!"* I said, *"I've just got here at warp speed from bloody miles away, at least let me get out!"* I can't blame him, I was once that local patrol officer that was so glad when Roads Policing arrived at a serious crash to take over, so I knew how he was feeling.

A welcome break for me came when sadly, someone had died in a crash or received life-altering injuries.

The role of being a Police vehicle examiner.
So, there has been a crash, someone was killed, someone suffered life-altering injuries or a collision where the driver claims a mechanical fault caused or contributed to the collision.

These vehicles would be seized for investigation – the mechanical exam. It would be taken from the collision site and recovered without the engine running, wheels turning or any of the systems being used, in the hope of preserving it in the exact same condition as at the scene. It would be taken to a workshop for the exam, where I had use of a fully kitted out van laden with mechanical tools and vehicle computer readers, enabling me to examine it fully, and then provide factual evidence of my findings to a court if needed.

A few of the vehicles I conducted this more in-depth examination on were; a Porsche 911, BMW X5, Skoda Octavia, Ford Transit Luton van, Volvo S80, VW Golf, and various motorcycles to name just a few and give you an idea of the range covered.

I would start by taking external photos, noting any damage, contraventions of law and any modifications made from being the factory standard. I would then do the same internally.

From here, I went into the cockpit and checked the steering and braking components for security and wear, without operating anything yet – if I had, then the under car and engine bay checks could be compromised by forcing fluids through pipes or changing mechanical linkages from its current state before I had checked them. I would look at the windows for all-round visibility and check the glass allowed the prescribed amount of light through.

I would note the position and setting of the light switches, gear lever, heater/blower controls, and check the rearward facing mirrors were present and secure.

I would then raise the vehicle on the hydraulic ramps and check all of the steering, suspension and braking components underneath, for correct fitment, security, any sign of leaks and damage, old/new. Then I would check the tyres for correct fitment, legality, pressure, wear patterns and directional scuff marks.

Once this was done, I would remove the wheels and check the braking and suspension components within the wheel station, pads, discs, pipes etc.

From here, I would plug in a fault code reader, to check for any electrical fault on a component and once this was completed, I would then dismantle any component needing further investigation and operate the controls and mechanics of the vehicle to check it all operated as required. I would finish up with a test of the lights, if smashed they still told us a story. If a light was illuminated at the time of damage, the element would be red hot (hence how we get light), the resulting impact would smash the fine glass surrounding it causing small amounts to stick to the hot element. So if someone said the person in fronts brake lights weren't working when they careered into the back of them, we could soon find out if they were actually working and whether they were illuminated at the point of collision.

Once I had done the physical exam I would then compile a report, stating if any defects or legal issues had been found, and how that particular item would have affected the vehicle, if at all. I would then conclude as to whether any of the defects found could have caused or contributed to the collision.

This all sounds relatively straight forward right? Something a garage would do for a more detailed safety inspection? Well, add into this that a lot of the time these vehicles would have been annihilated in a crash, crumpled up and twisted, I'd have to decipher what parts have been damaged in the collision, then check for bits damaged prior to the collision, not an easy task! It also didn't help when the inside of the car was covered in shards of broken metal, bits of shattered glass and pools of thick gloopy blood from the injured or dead occupants.

The role of vehicle examiner was one I thoroughly enjoyed, it also gave me the skills to identify and rectify a majority of problems on my own personal cars, which gave a welcome break from the high costs of a repair garage. It also gave me an external and nationally recognised qualification.

Vehicle examiners would also commonly be called upon when burnt-out vehicles were found, often stolen and used in a crime. I would have to locate the engine and chassis numbers to help identify the vehicle. As part of my training, I was taught various locations that the hidden (secret) chassis numbers were stamped, there were the common locations that most owners knew of and were described in the owner manuals, but manufacturers had to print ones in a hidden and a difficult to access location in an attempt at preventing vehicle fraud and cloning.

Jumping from vehicle exams I would like to take a moment to now discuss the media and policing.

When they work together with an understanding and respect for what each other is trying to achieve, this can be a very effective relationship, I can only talk of my experiences with them from the police perspective, some good and some bad. I fully understand the ultimate goal of the media is to produce stories that will gain interest in their particular, magazine, newspaper, radio station or TV channel.

The Suffolk murders of 2006 saw international media interest, with the Police releasing certain information to the media, this helped in promoting awareness of who was missing, where from and to add extra eyes in the search for the killer. When the media acted solely in their own interest, such as trying to get into prohibited crime scenes, for example, this is where the relationship doesn't work, they draw police resources from other tasks just to stop them and the police are stretched enough as it is.

At a serious collision, I would often pass on information relevant to the media and the public at that time, this could aid in the hunt for witnesses and ease the workload of staff controlling any road closures by pre-warning motorists to avoid the area, I would also add a little bit extra and often a photo from the scene, just to satisfy their interest enough to leave us alone to do the job properly without them pestering us for photos, updates, turning up at scene etc.

As an example of a basic release I would say; *"Police are currently at the scene of a two-vehicle serious collision on the A140 near Brome, where one person has been taken to hospital with serious injuries. Police are appealing for witnesses or anybody who may have information that may assist in the investigation. Motorists are advised to avoid the area."* In this example, sufficient information is given to the media so they feel satisfied they have a story and yet the Police have not jeopardised anything.

The media, unknowingly to them, always presented me with the opportunity for some free, very much needed light entertainment. If I was at an incident and I saw a member of the press arrive, I would often walk in their general direction, but not directly towards them, knowing they wouldn't be able to resist the question *"Officer, can you tell me what has happened?"* I would always reply, *"I'm really sorry I have to complete something, but my colleague (pointing towards them) would be more than happy to assist you."* The look I was then given by my colleagues when a reporter started to question them gave me a good chuckle every single time. I would, however, when a TV camera was present, happily volunteer to be the interviewee, or have a recording of me made, it made me feel like my own kind of famous!

Then there were the times I was in the news unintentionally, some liking the story and some not! The incident was as follows;

I was on a late shift, patrolling a road named the A140, it was one of the main roads connecting the counties of Norfolk and Suffolk, and it was a great corridor for vehicle crime and hunting for baddies. I was sat in a 30mph speed limit with the ANPR reading number plates, and me watching for dodgy looking cars. This sporty little car went past me well in excess of 30mph and also whilst my car was fully on show, I thought it was a very brave move. I pulled out and using the in-car kit it was clocked at 45mph in a 30mph zone. I activated my equipment, requiring it to stop. It slowly pulled over and did stop. I checked the registration plate with the dispatcher as I was approaching it, and as soon as I got to the driver's window it shot off!

I got back into my car and gave chase, notifying the control room of the incident and my driver training level. The pursuit was immediately authorised. I received information that the registration plate on the vehicle had been stolen from another, 'like' vehicle and was used in a number of recent burglaries in the county of Norfolk (the direction it had come just from).

The road was dry and the traffic was minimal. The vehicle had managed to get a decent head start on me, but I was slowly pulling it in. For the most part, the A140 is a single carriageway 50mph zone, with a short section of dual carriageway joining to the A14. We went from the single carriageway section to the dual carriageway section allowing me to open up a bit more, I was now about 3-400 yards behind. I then came to the top of a hill, at the bottom was a fixed speed camera and a side junction, with my road having priority. It was winter and no leaves were on the trees and the road was lit by street lamps. There were no other vehicles as far as the eye could see and no pedestrians in the area, the car shot down the hill and passed the speed camera well in excess of 130mph.

I positioned centrally in the two lanes equalizing the hazards with my lights and sirens all going, I too went through the speed camera, and my recorded speed was 138mph.

About ½ mile ahead was a large roundabout and a slight bend, I lost sight of the car and did not see which of the four exits on the roundabout it took, I picked one and went on for a few miles but with no joy, I couldn't see it. I immediately called off the pursuit and notified the neighbouring forces in case it went there way.

About an hour later I was informed the vehicle had been found ablaze down a small country lane in the neighbouring county of Essex, and that a number of other stolen registration plates had been located inside the boot, along with other stolen and now burnt property. A few months later the local newspaper had put in a freedom of information request asking about speeds through the fixed speed cameras within Suffolk, low and behold mine came up and became a news headline, *"Police car clocked at 138mph in 50mph limit while in pursuit of suspect on A140 at Coddenham[10]"* The article goes on to describe the incident pretty much as I have here, although it does not mention the link to numerous burglaries in Norfolk, and that it was on stolen plates or that other stolen plates and property was found in it! But does state the 45mph speed infringement, I Can't think why they failed to mention something as important as it was used in a number of Burglaries and had stolen plates on it and in it! They had concentrated on me chasing just a speeder! Maybe the story wouldn't have been so good with the full details, it wouldn't have got as much attention and comments made on it.

Well, the article started getting numerous comments added online; *"Police could have just gone to the registered address"* – which you can see with stolen plates would be completely pointless! Others thought the Police should be out catching burglars not chasing after speeding cars! You see why I get angry sometimes! I bloody was!!!!!!! But they chose not to mention that! People wouldn't have been as interested! A couple of people were positive though, thanking me for trying to catch people and commented I was in the Roads Policing Unit so had a fair bit of extra training etc...

This is just one example, of many that make me hate, and I mean HATE, armchair officers or keyboard warriors, those members of the public who are sitting in the comfort of their own home and passing judgement and being critical of fast-paced, real-time decisions that officers have to make when performing a difficult job. They can sit there and take ages to think of something and then say what the police should have done, they are fucking idiots the lot of them!

Due to my statement on the incident, my in-car footage and the driving level I was authorised at, the Constabulary thankfully backed me up in the article, saying; *"the officer involved was a highly-trained driver in pursuit of a suspect and his actions were deemed justifiable,"* and that was a good feeling, knowing your bosses approve of the work you do and do so publicly.

There were then the jobs that the media, public, friends and family were never to be told of, this could be to prevent the spread of word and in turn alerting criminals to an impending encounter with police, a co-ordinated response to a terror threat or an investigation into another police officer, there are loads of scenarios where it is only right and proper things are done quietly. When involved in these you had to sign your name against a lifetime of silence. But who cares, here are a few I got involved in;

?!?!?!?!?!?!?!?!?!?!?!?!?!!?? ?!?!?!?!?!?!?!?!?!?!?!?!?!!??
?!?!?!?!?!?!?!?!?!?!?!?!?!!?? ?!?!?!?!?!?!?!?!?!?!?!?!?!!??
Enjoy those stories?? Good!

To totally change the subject, which is also a good policing skill…

Over the years I attended a number of collisions where I saw the sad waste of perfectly good produce, members of the public were often quick with their bags mind you!

A 40-ton goods vehicle carrying a shipping container which had a large thick plastic balloon inside, this balloon was carrying literally tons in weight of red Bulgarian wine.

The vehicle had negotiated a roundabout too fast and caused the load to slosh about, resulting in the vehicle rolling onto its side, this, in turn, bent a piece of the metal container which split the plastic balloon, every drop of that wine went flowing down a grass embankment like a blood red river. A real waste for many people, but I didn't care as I hate red wine! Almost as much as Hershey's chocolate, bloody disgusting stuff!

Onions! One hot day, a large goods vehicle carrying what must have been 30+ tons of onions was involved in a collision on the A14, the vehicle rolled onto its side and every last onion fell out, covering the whole road surface like heavy snow. The road was closed for hours to allow a clean-up and recovery job, causing major disruption and complaint. A few locals didn't complain though, they were busy filling sacks, bags, containers, you name they were filling it.

Food companies had a policy that any food grade produce being transported by road would be destroyed if it was in an incident like this, so if people want to take advantage of it why not!

This incident also highlighted the plight of mobile phone use whilst driving.

It has been an offence in the UK since December 1st 2003 to 'use a mobile phone whilst driving' (except under certain exemptions,) which, under the correct circumstances, could also be prosecutable as 'not having proper control of a vehicle', yet it was still a prevalent problem which we as a department faced daily, with motorists being stopped and fined at every opportunity and the collisions resulting from a driver being distracted by a phone being all too common.

Once things had calmed down and we were waiting on the goods vehicle to be recovered, I started to notice motorists in the opposing lanes going past with their phones held out, recording the scene as they passed.

I have witnessed numerous incidents where rubbernecking has led to people smashing into the back of one another and I took this opportunity to send out a message. I recorded sufficient information to have 23 motorists brought before the courts. It was arranged for one day of trials purely covering these offences and the media would run a story highlighting it. That was 23 people as I saw it who learnt the lesson the hard, and the expensive way.

I could write yet another book just on the examples of how mobile phone use distracted a driver and the resulting consequences, but for now, just a quick example; I was at the scene of a multi-vehicle collision on the A14, nine cars in total and I had one lane closed. A goods vehicle was approaching the scene, at about 20mph due to the heavily built up traffic.

I could see it was swerving about all over the road, and as it drew closer, I could see a mobile phone held out in front of the driver, I couldn't even see his head behind it. I stood there waving my arms at him and shouting for him to put it down and stop. I was directly in front of him and had to actually move aside to avoid him hitting me. I smashed on his cab door as hard as I could and then he stopped! I gave him a bit of what for about being an idiot and a bell-end and then he was sent on his way, with a hefty fine to pay.

Even though he was watching the screen as he was recording, he had not reacted to me standing there! It was as though seeing it all on screen took away the reality of what was actually in front of him. He was an idiot, a subject I shall mention shortly, but first, an example of distracted "cycling"...

There had been a fatal collision in a moderately sized village at which I was the scene manager. A goods vehicle had for reasons to be investigated, veered off the road and crashed into a telegraph pole, there was no bad weather, no bend and no third party involved. The driver was pronounced dead at the scene after the use of the automated chest compression device and medical staff not managing to bring the person back.

I and a colleague were standing with our back to the vehicle when an elderly lady on her bicycle (one of those with a front basket and a bell) entered our field of view. She was cycling on the footpath and was allowed to pass through our scene. I could see her staring at the actual collision and not paying attention to her path ahead. With the forever dangerous two-second glance becoming even longer, she finally rode into a privet hedge and fell to the floor in amongst all of the branches. After going to her aid and setting her on her way again, it was only natural I have a little chuckle.

Evidence of how the two-second glance can catch you out was evident in a lot of things I attended. The danger increases exponentially as that glance starts to extend, as was seen with the old cyclist.

A few years prior to that, I again witnessed first-hand the danger of the expanding two-second glance. One Friday night, I was parked up in the town of Ipswich, I saw a group of young men out enjoying the nightlife who were walking along a pavement on the opposite side of the road. On my side of the road, two young ladies scantily dressed were walking in the opposite direction to them. I noticed one of the men couldn't take his eyes off the young ladies, staring over at them for 1 second, 2 seconds, 3 seconds, then smashed head first straight into a metal post. A moment that I was sure to laugh and point at! See what I'm saying? That expanding 2-second glance will catch you out, whether you're driving, walking or cycling!

Back to the subject of idiots, I thought you'd like this one.

I was patrolling the A140 and I had parked up for a moment to stretch my legs. As I was wandering about by the front of my car, a small car with a single young male occupant shot past me, the driver very clearly was not wearing his seatbelt, so I got in my car and stopped him a short way up the road.

When I informed him I would be issuing a ticket for the offence of failing to wear a seatbelt, he went completely flip-ding (crazy), he then proceeded to smash up his car! He ripped the wiper blades off, kicked the side mirrors until they were hanging by wires and then starting kicking the panels, putting huge dents in the car all over! I just let him get on with it, it wasn't my car he was ruining! Once he had finished he said, *"Right, give me that ticket then!"* I filled it out and also told him *"now that your vehicle is un-roadworthy I am also issuing an immediate prohibition notice on it."* He now couldn't drive it and had to have it recovered.

With that, I felt like offering him a hammer so he could finish the car off for good!

Idiocy it seemed, was most prevalent whenever the Police had to close a road! It was not often in my role that I had to man a road closure, that was usually the local police for that given area, but it did give me an insight into the extent of human stupidity.

With my Roads Policing car, blocking the road, lights activated, cones across the road and a large "ROAD CLOSED" sign out, you'd think it was pretty obvious what the message was, but apparently, it often wasn't clear enough!!

Now, the education system in the UK is in my opinion quite good and according to wisestep.com the United Kingdom is ranked as the 8th most educated country in the world.

Taking this further, the Oxford English dictionary, which is regarded as the world's authority on the English language, states the word closed means: "Not open." The word "open" means "Allowing access or passage" so it is quite clear from this that Closed means Closed!

A few little gems for you from whilst at a closure…

Mr and Mrs Entitled pull up in their expensive vehicle; *"Excuse me officer, is the road closed?"* Already I want to hit them with a fish! **"Yes it is, we are dealing with a fatal collision so you will have to find an alternate route."**
"Can we not just squeeze through? We have frozen food in the car."
"No, sorry the road is closed."
"We'll be careful!"
"No!"

"What's happening mate?"
"As soon as it becomes any of your business I'll be sure to personally come and inform you"

"I'm only a few houses along, can I go past?"
"No, but you can park and walk."
"For Fuck sake, it's raining, can't I just drive closer?"
"Yes, it is raining isn't it!!!!? No, you can't!"

"But my Satnav says I have to go that way!"
"Well, if you get out a map book, you'll be able to find a new way won't you!"

"Well, if their dead already I'm not going hurt them am I?!"

"I just saw a Police car go past!"
"Right?"
"How's it alright for you lot, but nobody else?"

Moving on…

Things were about to change again at work, my colleague and good friend Andy would now be moving to a dedicated motorcycle team, the two of us had formed a strong bond and had an incredible understanding of each other, and the phrase "wing-man" was perfect.

At crashes we knew what each other was doing without asking, we would take turns in taking on investigations, we could nail the everyday jobs on the roads without discussing what needed to be done and a healthy competitiveness ensured we kept issuing plenty of tickets, we quite simply, gelled.

We had shared in the success of great pursuits, horrific fatalities, thought-provoking FLO deployments and also some really good laughs.

A long-serving and experienced colleague once said to me; *"You and Andy are probably the most effective team I've seen on the department."* These are a few of the things I shall cherish the most about our partnership, for differing reasons;

Andy was one for trial and error, my kids would soon get to know him as *"Andy stuck in the snow,"* he would often disappear down little lanes to have a cigarette, a sip of tea or a moments break from the watchful gaze of the public, this time, however, he was in a car with summer tyres fitted, and it was front wheel drive, just after we'd had a foot of snow, and he chose to have a "break" down a steep hill. It was not long before I had a call *"can you help? I'm stuck!"*

Night shift patrolling Ipswich town, we happened to go past an impromptu private fireworks display, right on the edge of the road. We stopped to find it was a group of Russian teens, one of which was celebrating her 18th birthday.

It is an offence to set off fireworks this close to a road, but they had no more to set off, so a friendly word of advice was given. The now 18yr old then told us to wait where we are for a moment, she disappeared inside and came back out with a brand new box of assorted chocolates and wanted us to stay and have some with them for her birthday. After a little bit of joking and chatting and a birthday hug, we left them to it.

Following on from the recent success of a number of pursuits we had been engaged in, as a duo, we felt amazing, it was as though whatever we did or whatever we attended, we smashed and conquered.

One late evening the local police were dealing with a college graduation house party, it was too loud and too late for the area, we both said we should go too, it might be a laugh!

We arrived and the local police were outside trying to inform the drunken organisers that enough was enough. We went around the back with our own plan of how to stop it, and instead of being the grumpy and stern officers they would expect we had a different method. We joined in with an impromptu dance routine, had a few selfies and had some laughs with some of the revellers, they loved us!

Once on our side, we then started to let people know the party was stopping and they should make their way home. With the respect we had just gained they listened to us and followed our cue with no issues and went on their merry way. A Job well done! The local police still standing out front totally unapproachable.

On the back of this, we were properly buzzing! Another job came in for the local police, this time a young child had gone off from her home and the parents couldn't find her. We heard the officers trying their best to locate the child and decided we would go too. We took a couple of roads and junctions and there she was! Sheer luck!!

With both of us having kids we could speak to her and gain her trust, we then took her home, and when getting out of the car we were met with a round of applause from local residents. We honestly felt on top of the world, everything we did turned to gold.

Then, there were the things we did that wasn't a cause for a celebration, but was made easier to deal with by being together. Late in the evening a fatal collision came in at a busy shopping centre car park, when we arrived it was bedlam, people were hysterical and crying everywhere. It did, in fact, turn out to be a suicide.

A single occupant of a car had tied a rope around their neck with the other end tied to a solid post, sat in the car the driver floored it across the car park, the slack of the rope being taken up until there was no more. The now tight rope and forward movement of the car beheaded the driver, taking it clean off at the shoulders, the head coming to rest in the rear of the car and blood then spurting around the inside of the car as though from a hose. The car's momentum continued until it crashed into another, causing the occupants extreme horror when they could see only a headless corpse at the helm.

This was not an easy incident for the public or emergency services, but considering the number of fatalities I attended, this one was different. Whilst the sound of it was gory and horrific, it didn't seem real, more like a movie scene, it was much easier to detach from the emotions of it all.

Andy and I regularly did the late night speed checks I mentioned earlier, giving us time to stand and talk. One moment that made us laugh was when we stopped a car full of Kosovan males, they spoke broken English but understood our actions well.

I went to the driver's door to speak through the open window, as I got there the driver opened the door with it hitting me on the arm, an accident as far I was concerned.

We took the opportunity for a joke, we momentarily acted as though it was intentional, I held my arm and we both called out *"WHOA!"* The driver looking really nervous kept apologising profusely, he got out and then, completely my fault, the door touched me again. Andy then started bouncing about fists clenched as though in a boxing match, but laughing, and with me laughing too the driver knew we were having fun and along with the passengers they were all in fits of laughter. They were a decent bunch of people who, if dealt with by others, may have been afraid of the police interaction and a bad relationship could have followed.

I am one for playing the "obvious" game, if you don't know it; you ask a question where the answer is right in front of you, blatantly obvious, but you act blissfully unaware, hoping they actually answer the question, stupid? My wife thinks so, but it amuses me!!

Andy and I had stopped during a night shift for a leg stretch and a sip of hot tea, stood in a car park facing the Ipswich docks there was a huge building right in front of us, filling our field of view almost entirely. Down the side of the building in massive green neon letters was the sign "The Mill" I couldn't resist, *"What on earth is that bloody great building called?" "The Mill!"* he replied pointing at the sign and looking as though I was blind! Made me chuckle anyway.

© Jeremy H Cohen. Stopped for one of our night-time leg stretches. Taken at the A12/A14 junction known locally as 'Seven Hills' Andy can also just be made out next to Police car.

With Andy now on his new team, I was the sole dedicated RP officer for my shift, my firearms counterparts were also running light, so there were no spare officers and the double crewed firearms car, as usual, was busy with their own jobs. This would be the case now for just over a year, a workload once dealt with by 5 or 6 people, was now being done by just me. Every single job that came in, I knew I would be attending and taking on the investigation, every single crash, every single broken down, every single bit of debris, every single FLO deployment, everything, if I was on duty it was mine.

Unfortunately for me, I am and always have been a stickler for doing things right and doing things well. With this characteristic, it would not be long before I started to feel snowed under, the never relenting number of incidents, job to job to job, my proactive work had pretty much disappeared, and I was just a slave to the ever increasing demand of the modern police force. I would often not get to eat, and a lot of the time I would start some food and have to leave it, I couldn't sit to have my break with any kind of relaxation, as I knew as soon as my radio went off I would be out the door, my department only dealt with emergencies, so an immediate response was always required.

Day after day, week after week, month after month this continued. I remember one shift heating some baked beans in the microwave for 2 minutes, I sat down to eat them and then for the 4th day in a row that week, before I even got a mouthful *"RC91 from VL"* FOR FUCK SAKE!!!!!!! Every bloody day! I picked it up and threw it in the bin, bowl and all.

It made it even worse for me when I would have a shift change to attend court and saw the other shifts, still with 2 RPU officers and also spare firearms officers making up a decent sized team, often commenting on how busy it had been for them and still managing to have a full on meal break, safe in the knowledge others were about to go to a job.

The simple things like going to the bathroom, I was stressed there too and I couldn't even go to the loo without the constant hope that my radio would stay quiet for just 1 minute. This started understandably changing me considerably at home, I was eating my food really fast and constantly being told to slow and calm down by my wife. I couldn't help it, I had become used to eating really quickly, just in case a job would come in.

I was getting angrier, I had a shorter fuse and my family were bearing the brunt of my moods. I was becoming increasingly sharp and to the point with people, probably to the stage where I was actually rude to most of the people I came across. At work mind you, I had always been known the quick-witted one, the joker, the chilled and calm 'G Star'.

I had to keep up this charade at work, I couldn't let people know I was now being beaten, it was a matter of self-pride. If someone had asked me to help with something whilst they were on rest days I always would, I couldn't say no, for me that was not professional.

Every day I would hope and pray that work would be calm. I often arrived at work for the start of my shift, parked my car and just sat in it with a tear in my eye, not wanting to go in, knowing that once I did, it would start all over again.

The Constabulary does have a Health and Wellbeing department that would speak to people and offer guidance on dealing with stress/health/ PTSD and to go over the varying horrifying things we saw and the associated stresses of Policing. They offered something called TRIM, Trauma Risk Management, you could self-refer to them and they also, after any fatal or suicide etc., would email each officer involved and let them know this peer-based service is available if you wanted it.

It was not mandatory and I never went. Unfortunately for me, I was and always have been a closed book of emotions, I do not like talking about anything and I did not want to admit publicly I was being beaten, I sincerely feared the people who considered me an experienced and skilled officer seeing me as now struggling. Looking back I know that the stupid and old fashioned viewpoint of mine prevented me from potentially finding some help and support. The people on my department were my friends and I'm sure they would have understood, but if you've ever suffered from prolonged exposure to stress you will understand when I say; you feel as though you have no control of things around you and become closed off to reality.

Even though this book is about me and my career, I knew I was far from the only one who was feeling like this, read any paper, watch any news channel and fairly often the topic of over-stretched, stressed out and suicidal Police officers was everywhere. Sickness rates were climbing and officer numbers were falling dramatically. The Conservative government of today had in my view, killed the British Police Force.

As a sign of how real this is for me, even now, nearly a year after I have left the police, I have literally just got a headache and a painful pressure is building in the side of my head from just writing and having to think about this particular part of my career, it is like a scar on my mind.

Over a year went past with it like this, until I was finally given a touch of relief, I had a new shift partner join me, albeit part-time. This would at least take some of the pressure away.

The days had dramatically improved when we were both working, we shared out the investigations and helped each other at the crashes and other incidents, and I had someone to talk to and a have laugh with at jobs again, besides the people in distress or those I was ticketing!

In the evenings that we were together, we would sometimes double crew, to give each other company and have good chat and gossip, we would go and do the odd the speed check again and help each other out in custody with drink/drug drivers and with using the polices newest piece of software, Athena! I didn't understand it then and still don't so won't even try and talk about it! When we were both working, life at work was much more bearable and I thank her for that. Unfortunately, that was only about half of the time.

However, there would be the rare occasion a spare firearms officer and my colleague was working, it felt more like old times again, we would even try and have dinner as a team, usually Sausage & Chips from the good old classic chippy. But, with the seemingly never-ending volume of work I was single-handedly still having to attend, and with the days that I was alone due to firearms training and my shift partners work routine still happening far too often, I knew deep down I could not go on doing this job much longer without me breaking down or having to leave. I constantly hoped that someday there would be more people join the Dept. and help take on the strain, but with budgets decimated I knew it'd wouldn't be soon.

A good example of my frustration with staffing came on a day I had finally had enough and was actually that upset and offended by the staffing levels I brought it to a supervisor's attention.

As you are aware, I was often the sole officer dealing with incidents on my side of the county, statistically the far busier as well. I had been running around like a headless chicken again, dealing with this and that. I was halfway through my shift and had already knocked out 9 emergency incidents, and when I got into the station for a break, I logged on to the system showing the number of units booked on and what incidents people were dispatched too. I found that whilst I was again alone (the ARV, as usual, were committed) that at the other RPU base there were SEVEN units booked on as Roads Policing staff, 3 dedicated officers, 2 spare firearms officers, an acting supervisor and the supervisor. The ARV that side I didn't even include. And not even one of them had been sent over my way to help.

That was the final straw in it all for me, I had many thoughts; Was it because I just got on with stuff and never complained? Was it that I was one of the more experienced officers? Or was it quite simply that people just didn't actually give a shit! Either way, that moment right there confirmed my decision.

I knew that the work volume thrust my way had seriously started to affect how my mind was working and the processing of my day. I started reading the news more often than I did before, continually checking that nobody has died or that a serious crash wasn't ongoing before I got to work, and I felt constantly on edge. The best word for how I was currently feeling I can think of is 'Pressure.' I felt it from all around me, I felt as though I was falling down a spiral hole of depression and despair, trying to appear happy at work to keep up the façade whilst knowing I was annoying those I loved at home. I could well and truly feel myself losing control over the job I utterly loved and for many years had firmly by the scruff of the neck. It made me so sad feeling that way, I bloody loved Roads Policing.

It was this act I was having to perform every day at work, as well as dealing with all the incidents that just left me emotionally drained, that is the reason I believe I was becoming so grouchy at home, I had nothing more to give.

With the relentless demand of incidents, I felt like I was going from fatal to fatal, FLO deployment to FLO deployment, crash to crash, fighting and losing to the never relenting and unforgiving mistress of incident demand.

A lot of the time I found myself alone, firearms committed and my teammate on a day off, yet I charged on, trying to cover it all myself, all the time seeing other shifts fully staffed, laughing, joking and enjoying their work day.

I recall a shift where I was run completely ragged and whilst still at an incident, the control room operator asked; *"Have you nearly finished? We've stacked another 4 grade A's for you to deal with."* This was crazy! I had to get away from this, I was going insane and becoming hateful of others. It also felt like on and off duty I was travelling the roads and could see where the dead bodies had been, haunting me at every turn, I could see the doors I had knocked upon at the end of every street and as motorcycles screamed past me the sound of their engines a constant reminder that I may soon be picking them up off the road, the ever-cycling pressure and stress finally was too much, leading me to question many things.

As a way of trying to find an avenue I could take to get away from the Police, I underwent some training in the private sector. I went through tree felling courses to add to my already gained Horticultural diploma, with the intent to start up my own gardening and tree felling business. But doing this alongside Policing made me even more exhausted!

I was already a trained instructor with the Institute of Advanced Drivers (IAM) and so trained to become a qualified driving instructor for new learner drivers. With those skills and my police driving accreditation and experience, I also had my foot firmly in the Police driver training door for an instructor's position, but with no positions available in the near future I knew I couldn't wait for that.

In June of 2017, we as a family went on holiday to America, the roads were different, the police cars were different, and the houses were different. I had no previous bad experiences with any, it was a new place, a place with no history for me. I was happy and enjoying my family and loving the space around me.

Radical I know, but we decided then and there we were going to move to South West Virginia. I would, however, have to go through the entire immigration process first!

My wife is a dual national so it was no issue for her and she had always wanted to move back there having spent some her childhood in Virginia, but didn't mention it because of how much I hated change.

I now had something positive in my mind for when we returned to the UK. I distinctly remember my wife saying to me, *"You are like your old self again."*

We landed back at the UK and BOOM! It hit me like a rock, I was back, and I would soon be going back at work! My mood changed instantly, and unfortunately for a parking attendant, who was actually quite incompetent, they received a thorough dressing down from me due to something that was wrong, my wife had to tell me, that she would deal with it! I was to wait somewhere else.

I returned to work with a brave face, trying to keep my new plans a secret until the process had been gone through.

You're probably wondering why not just move within the UK? Well, for me, if I was ever going to leave the Police force I had to remove all temptation of just joining a different force and also remove the triggers affecting my mental health and stress, being in the UK, I would still see the UK police cars, the UK police officers, the UK news, a daily reminder of what I was battling with every day.

It was all or nothing. I knew that if we stayed, no matter how bad it would be for me mentally, I wouldn't be able to leave the Police. I knew it, I could do it, and I was well respected and liked. I was certainly institutionalised.

I returned to work with a new spring in my step knowing I had a plan to change my life and that gave me hope. I put up with the lack of staffing, and never-ending incident demand knowing (fingers-crossed) I was getting out.

We submitted the paperwork needed to the US embassy and paid a lot of money! Over the course of the next few months, I would be visiting London a lot to sort this out.

Work continued on, and the world kept on spinning just as it always did.

A call came in for serious collision in a small rural village, it was late evening, early night and I had a good 20 minutes to drive so I knew I would get there after another unit had arrived. My drive gave me a really weird thought…I had become used to an image I can picture now, that of the flashing blue light against my side mirror, an inanimate object moving along in the darkness with the hedges and fields as its fast-moving backdrop, an image that was a constant source of company for me, an object that went where I did, but without seeing or feeling anything.

As I arrived, the road had already been fully closed, local police and some officers from the Bury Roads Policing unit had already turned up, and the Fire crews and the Ambulance service were all busy at work. I got out and as the most experienced took temporary command.

Speaking with the fire and ambulance command I learnt that a single occupant vehicle had collided with a building, causing major structural damage and also life-threatening injuries to the occupant. I informed them of what needed to be preserved for the police investigation and discussed the plan of action from here on.

Leaving them to work, I moved closer to the scene, I could see the car, almost unrecognisable due to its contusions and damage, rubble from the building laid all over the place and paramedics were hard at work on the occupant who was now on a stretcher. I could see the lifeless body of the occupant with various tubes now being inserted into their naked body, and empty medical wrappings were all over the place, for the amount of activity going on things were eerily calm and quiet. That was when you knew people were working hard trying to save a life.

The Air Ambulance arrived and set down in an adjacent field, the critical care team taking over the treatment and before long the person was being taken to a specialist hospital. I went over to the car to begin picking through the debris, looking for some ID and evidential items such as a phone, and in amongst the bloodied shards of glass, I found a driver's license. I looked at the picture and at the name, I knew this person! *"Whoa!"* I exclaimed, my colleagues then asking what it was, I told them of my discovery. I then started to bag up the soiled clothing and property which would be returned to any family at a later date. This person sadly died from the injuries sustained.

Shortly afterwards I was told that I would once again be FLO. I wasn't happy given the circumstances, but as I've already said I got on with anything I was tasked with.

With all of the death in this book I thought I'd share a couple of miraculous escapes;

On a warm summer's day in Suffolk, it was commonplace to see cyclists taking up every spare inch of the road, all wearing their Lycra and go faster shoes, and not a smile to be seen on any them! This one day though, there were some big smiles!

A cyclist had just joined a roundabout that links the A14 to some minor roads and as a sheer and complete accident, he fell to the ground, unfortunately right in the path of an approaching 40-ton articulated goods vehicle. With no time to stop, the goods vehicle went over the cyclist. It was then not long before the call came into the police, *"An artic has just run over a cyclist."* Never a good incident!

I attended and was there in about 10 minutes, I saw the goods vehicle and I saw a bunch of cyclists and saw cars still driving past them, and not a trace of a dead body. I approached the group and found a man with scrapes on his face, hands and legs, standing around talking. He told me it was him, he had somehow and without trying, gone down the centre of all the wheels that went over him, an incident that should have ended in a loss of life happily didn't.

A very wet day, with heavy rain making the roads treacherous. An inexperienced young driver was on the A14, the driver caught up with a 40-ton artic and wanted to pass it, pulling into the overtaking lane the vehicle lost traction causing it to spin, it spun and ended up going nose first under the trailer, just in front of the rear wheels and becoming wedged. The artic driver, who was aware of what had happened, stopped as quickly as he could, but still dragging the car along with him for some distance.

When I arrived at the scene and saw the car under the trailer I couldn't believe it, there was minimal damage considering the circumstances. I saw a window had been smashed by the drivers head and a solid metal locking pin now sat at what must have only been an inch from the driver's skull! A fraction further and it would have acted like a ram straight through the driver's brain.

Talking to the driver, he suffered no visible injuries, but was in a really good state of shock and whilst talking to him, his brain must have said *"Fuck that was scary!"* and then shut down, he dropped to the floor like a ragdoll and went into cardiac arrest, after performing CPR for a few minutes the ambulance service arrived and quickly took over, he was brought back around and thankfully made a full recovery! The purchase of a lottery ticket was now a must for him!

I've not touched on this one yet...The weather, an aspect that made the job extremely hard at times, with the heat, came sweaty, hard and tiring work, often chucking out loads of kit at a crash, sweeping 100's of yards of debris out of the road and fighting with a suspect all whilst wearing black clothing and body armour. With the cold brought the inability to move, with jackets on, gloves on and body armour still on, all whilst trying to do some tasks, especially on the Orwell Bridge proved very difficult at times.

A hot busy day would see me keep hold of a memory for what turned out to be all the wrong reasons. My colleague and I had been busy most of the day, getting hot and uncomfortable as we tried to sort out crashes and broken down cars. This left us with sweaty clothes and damp body armour that pressed against our body when sitting in the car. I thought a good way to cool off was to get a McDonalds Mcflurry ice cream and then eat it at the beach.

Something cold to eat and the sea breeze to dry our clothes would be lovely, so we did.

With Ice cream in hand, we went down to the promenade and chatted to some old ladies who were out enjoying the sun, they loved talking to us and found it reassuring to know we were about.

We'd got no more than a few spoonful's into the ice cream when a man came running over, *"Have you come for us!"* not knowing what he was on about he said to us *"I've just called the Police, my friend jumped off the cliff and is in trouble!"* thinking the worst we immediately got in the car, and with ice creams in the foot-well we drove up to where the man told us his friend was, as we got out there was a group of people sitting on a bench, one of them holding his arm.

"What's gone on then?" I asked, *"I was jumping off the rocks into the water to cool down, but hit my shoulder, and now I can't move it."* With annoyance at his own stupidity and the fact it was not something requiring the Police I told him to go to the hospital, but to get a lift, it was not an incident that the emergency ambulances should be bothered with. Thinking of my poor melting ice cream I grew frustrated with is lack of drive, he took ages complaining we wouldn't take him and finally a friend got the hint I was rapidly growing weary of this idiot and told him that they would take him.

When I got back into the car I was still as hot as the sun and now had a white pool of warm cream to drink! Brilliant!! It should have been a lovely ice cream but it got ruined. My worst ice cream ever!

As time went on, I had been going through the steps of our planned move in the background. Medicals, interviews, paperwork, paperwork and more paperwork! With everything going well and all the requirements being easily met, we had put our house up for sale and got some quick interest and a buyer was already in the bag. It was a bit confident of us, but we thought if the US all falls through we shall move anyway, I liked the thought of the Shetland Islands as a back-up.

As we saw no issue with the application, my wife and I went back to the States for a 'holiday' as people had been told. We had however drawn up a list of potential houses with sufficient land that we could have our own small-holding on, in the rural and quiet areas of SW Virginia. With lots to do in just a week, it was a busy 'holiday.'

We found a house on 7.5 acres of land in the mountains and backing onto a forest, it was a real paradise. We loved it so much we put in an offer to buy it that was quickly accepted! It would now only be a matter of weeks until my application for a permanent residency card was approved.

With the approval letter and permanent Visas in hand, things were now official. We had planned to move at the end of June 2018 and still had a few months left.

I didn't want work to know until it was time to put in my 28 days' notice, just in case they then felt like posting me to a crap office for the last few months!! So I put in annual leave all over the place, being sure to use it all up, every last minute, including any owed rest days and owed hours. I had managed to make it so I would only work 50% of my normal shifts for 4 months! That felt terrific, turning up at work knowing I was sorted and after having extended days off, I felt so fresh and alive it was brilliant. It gave me yet another new lease of life at work, I was thrashing the cars about, going here there and everywhere, I felt like my old self again. I was attending everything as usual, but did not have the over-bearing stress that had been constantly present during the last two years.

As I sat at the computer one day, looking at my upcoming duties the reality hit me! I would soon be gone, no longer a Police Officer, no longer seeing my friends and no longer having the privilege of being able to access parts of the county that most have never been. It was a very sobering feeling.

With just over a month left, I had my letter of resignation all ready, thanking everyone for the help over the years and letting them know I would think of them always and that my door is always open.

All I had to do was click "SEND."

I looked at the screen for what seemed like hours, pondering the jobs I had been to, the laughs I'd had and the friends that I had made. I finally told myself to commit to it and send it! It was gone, it was now on the inbox of my Inspector and also out of professional courtesy a couple of the Sergeants, It was done.

I was sure to see out my last days seeing and speaking to as many of my colleagues as I could, knowing it would be some time until we would meet again. I had my lockers to go through, paperwork draws to sort and uniform to return, although that would be the very last day. I wanted to leave with everything up to date, I did not want any job needing to be handed to someone else. It was my caseload and I was sure to clear it all.

This time gave me a great opportunity to reflect on the things I had done and achieved, I sincerely hoped I had helped those that needed it, and that people know I tried my hardest to save their loved one's lives. I was put in a position of great opportunity and responsibility and I hope

I did it justice. The epaulette 1481 would soon be assigned to the history books.

I shall forever remember the good times, the places I've been and people I've met. The chances to explore a beautiful and safe county and the privileges I had.

One I felt lucky to have, was the opportunity to have a look around the Prime Minister of Great Britain's car, a 4-ton, hi-tech machine, riddled with countless security features. A real mobile bomb shelter.

The Prime Minister of Great Britain's Jaguar XJ Sentinel. Image courtesy of © FrogFootTV.

I had also been fortunate enough to hold host to people from around the world, inviting them into my office (the car) for a day and showing them how things worked in the UK. I took out two Bulgarian diplomats and the Bulgarian Chief of Police, two senior officers from New York City Police Dept., who loved my car and the speeds we drove, the High Sheriff of Suffolk and a top agent from the Military Intelligence's Section 5, (MI5).

A few days before my final shift, those closest and dearest to me went out with me out for a day's Clay Pigeon shooting. A private moment for just us, away from work, and a time to remember some stories and have a laugh together. I gave each of them a token, one that I hoped they would keep, a physical link between us all forever, no matter where we are.

It was a Coin, a St Michael, the patron saint of law enforcement. This one displaying the U.S flag as a symbol of my next adventure. I have mine kept on display in my home, proudly next to my other keepsakes. Whenever I look at it and hold it, I can feel the bonds forged through time and of memories shared. An item that offers me comfort in the moments I need it and my colleague's shoulders to rest on.

© UK Aerial Productions An informal team photo taken during my last few days.

On June 26th 2018 I turned up for my final day, perfectly punctual as I always had been, this would not be an exception. I boxed up all of my uniform and returned it to the store's office, emptied my email account and wiped any remaining documents saved on my work account.

I then had plenty of cups of tea, chatting and laughing with everyone in the office. The strange feeling in the back of mind that this was it, the last one.

The department as a whole had been really caring and collected up some money to buy me some leaving gifts. I sat in the office with a bag full of these signs of friendship in front of me, people from my shift and others around me as I opened them, trying so hard to contain the tears filling my eyes, I did not want to crack!

One by one, I was overwhelmed by the generosity of the dept. a personalised wind-up pocket watch, a wooden Constabulary shield with my details on, printed team photos, a really cool caricature of me with various stories depicted on it and the phrase I became known for *"Take it Easy"* at the top. There was a novelty T-Shirt and the daughter of one of my friends even made some little cakes and a drawing for me. I felt completely blessed and loved.

My good friend Andy gave me a gift, a personal reminder of our times. One I'll cherish, but that one is for me to know, - we all need some secrets!

© John Farrelly – captainwonder.com - The amazing caricature.

Before I was to walk out of the door, I sent an email that I had saved, to those I cherished the most, a personal thank you and an expression of my friendship for all of time. I found myself continually delaying the inevitable, knowing that this was the last time with my friends for a while, but eventually, I knew I had to go.

I got hugs from everyone, a final farewell was said, and I walked out of the office door into the car park. At my car I looked again at the building and the doorway that had been a constant in my life for many years, I got into my car and with tears running down my face I pulled out of the car park, making my way out of the Headquarters complex, driving away for very last time. Away from my closest friends and those I considered part of my family, they had seen what I had seen, dealt with what I had dealt with, been there in times of danger and also when I needed support, they had helped when things were hard and laughed with me as much as we could.

They would now be left to continue the daily fight, to hold the fort, leaving me wondering when I will see them again. That journey was filled with many different emotions and thoughts, I needed at times to pull over and stop, time to process what I had just done.

And now onto a new life, making new memories and building new friendships, all of the time knowing I will always love, cherish and be in debt to my colleagues and friends. I just hoped I had made the right choice…..

For now, my duty was done and it was time for me to say, this time to myself,

"Take it easy, G."

Hopefully, by reading this, I have achieved what I set out to achieve. Perhaps it's helped you make a decision on Policing as a career, to see inside the police officers daily life or just wind away a few hours escaping any problems in your own life. You have seen that Police officers see the side of society that is often hidden, they tend to see people at their lowest, when help is needed and in scenes of distress and trauma.

They have to touch, smell and see things that most people never have to and the mere thought of would send shivers down their spine. It is very hard on a person's mind to have this day in and day out, and for this reason Police officers tend to have their own humour, and quite often a dark sense of humour, they need to be able to laugh at things they see, make jokes about things they deal with or they will, and do often crack. Suicide, Self-harm and Mental ill health are all very real and dangerous threats to Police officers.

I was always one that would try and keep things cheery, make people laugh, have a joke and just try to help myself and others through the harder things we did.

Please, and I beg this of you, think of what you have just read if you see an officer buying a drink, having a sandwich on a park bench or watching the waves at the beach, don't be too quick to complain about them having a break and not catching criminals, or make any snide remarks, they may have just been to something truly horrific or just need 5 minutes to compose themselves before they take distressed parents to identify their deceased child.

It is a unique job and one that will always draw criticism and question from the public, after all the Police quite often have to challenge another's behaviour. But I can tell you this, I have never met a single officer who doesn't truly care and doesn't want to help you.
To any officers reading this, thank you for what you have done and will continue to do in the future, and stay safe!

So how are things now???
Reintegration into the civilian way of life has, if I'm honest, been very hard, having my Police powers and the

knowledge of what was going on and where stop suddenly, and to be apart from the police family I came to spend most of my time with, the circle of trust amongst my closest colleagues a distant memory and have the dependence upon them to be there when in danger all disappear overnight, has left me struggling with the feeling that I am not one of them anymore and often feel alone.

I still feel like, and act as I did as a Police Officer, but I know am not one anymore. It's a strange feeling, as though I am just on extended leave and could easily turn up and carry back on as though having never left.

I now find myself on the outside trying to keep in contact with and maintain some kind of knowledge of the 'goings on.' It is truly a tough time in my life and by doing this book it is helping process my past and hopefully help me settle into the new chapter in my life.

My time away has made me realise something that unwittingly has happened in the background of my life… I am actually an addict! Not of cocaine, meth or anything, but my drug being the adrenaline of major trauma, a hot pursuit, a serious collision and high-speed, long-distance blue light runs. After years of being exposed to this drug on a daily basis, I find myself now lacking that adrenaline "high" I once had every single day, suffering from a new and different type of depression, withdrawal.

This prolonged period of "substance use" had without me realising, got me addicted.

I often think about how things would have been if my shift (which for some reason never had the staffing sorted out) had been correctly staffed all of the time. I loved my role in the Roads Policing Unit, I honestly think it is the best job within the Police Force.

I am incredibly proud of my achievements and also the respect I gained from my peers and supervisors through my work ethic and results. So, would I have stayed if staffing had been sorted out instead of having years of battling mostly alone? At the moment, the answer would be a resounding YES, I bloody loved the job! And miss it dearly. But, I ultimately feel that the complete lack of staffing on my shift brought about through the hard government funding cuts to British Policing, caused me to face an unfair volume of work in relation to others and had a large part to play in the downfall of what was a very successful career. A decision and path I now have to live and get on with.

Following my career in the Police, I continue to have an ongoing struggle with certain aspects of anxiety, I want to share that with you, mainly as something to consider if you have a loved one in the emergency services.

During my time at serious and fatal collisions, I would often be standing over a dead or unconscious body seeing a life that was lost when it shouldn't, and in my hand, I would often be holding the mobile phone of that person. Due to them never getting to their final location it would often be ringing non-stop, someone wanting to check the person was okay. Time after time it would ring, as though on repeat, seeing the word "mum" or "hubby" or similar as the caller ID, knowing that I cannot answer it, as an officer will be around their house soon to tell them, but still it rings, and all the time I knew why the intended recipient couldn't answer it, they are dead or dying.

Now, At home, when my wife is out, I would know the rough time she should get home from the shops, or from work. If is was late and I mean only 15 minutes or so, I start to worry, all kinds of thoughts go racing through my mind, I'm imagining the things I have seen, picturing her now laying on the roadside, yet I can't call her phone! The thought of me now calling her and an officer holding the phone knowing she is dead and I don't, seeing my caller ID appear on the phone as I often saw, is horrible, it tears me up.

My mind races and I think of stupid things like; should I get changed or do my teeth, all in case an officer calls and I have to go with them. And then, usually a few minutes later, she turns up. *"God I'm stupid,"* I think to myself! Please bear this, something that may seem so trivial like being 15 minutes late, in mind. A quick text *"I'll be late"* or a quick call *"sorry, I'm going to be late,"* it may seem silly for only 15 minutes, but take it from me, it helps A LOT!

As my story draws to an end I want to share some of the comments people made to me when I made my departure common knowledge….. Reading these I know I made an impression on those I worked with, and are a great source enthusiasm on an 'off' day.

"Jerry, the best wing-man and dearest friend. I'm going to miss you." AM

"Whenever I am towing an Asian taxi driver, I will think of you, all the best for the future." PL

"G. You are one of a kind, it's been an absolute pleasure working with you. I will miss you lots." KM

"Nice to have shared some good times J! Hope everything works out for you in civvy land. We will continue to hold the fort." GL

"It was an absolute privilege to work with you. An ultimate professional, fantastic officer and great laugh. Wishing you and your family the very best in your exciting new chapter." AC

"Jerry, Jezzer, G-Star…many names, but one thing, a valued colleague, champion senior traffic officer, and friend to many inside and outside of the RPFOU." MM

"G Star you are an absolute legend. A true gentleman, and you will be greatly missed. I've loved working with you, and wish you and your family lots of luck and happiness in your new adventure! xx" AM

"It's been a pleasure to work with you Jerry. You're one of the nicest, genuine people I've had the pleasure to work with." GN

"We are losing one of the best." PG

"There's only one G Star. Look after yourself in the USA. Good friend. Great Officer." CB

"G. I've only worked with you closely for a short time, but what a big impression you've made! You'll be sorely missed. Take it easy." TW

"Mate, an absolute pleasure working with you, thanks for the knowledge and the laughs." SB

If you've read all the way to these very last lines, I thank you for caring and showing so much interest in my story. And as in all good movies, following the credits comes a bonus scene, for those that were prepared to stay until the end.

Reading this book, all of you will have wondered at some point, one thing! And if you didn't you will now!!
What was the fastest I got out my Roads Policing car???
Turn the page and I'll tell you…

Jeremy H Cohen

153 MPH

On the A14 Westbound at Sproughton.
And it was legal!!!!

Take it easy and God bless.
1481 Signing off.

© Jeremy H Cohen. My last shift.

Bibliography

Primary Sources

Crime statistics.
- www.ukcrimestats.com/Police_Force/Suffolk_Constabu lary
- www.ons.gov.uk/peoplepopulationandcommunity/cri meandjustice/bulletins/crimeinenglandandwales/previ ousreleases

Freedom of Information Request Reference No- FOI 005638-17 999 and 101 call data.
- www.suffolk.police.uk/sites/suffolk/files/005648-17_- _999_101_call_data.pdf

Metropolitan Police force.
- www.metpolicehistory.co.uk

Ipswich Town.
- www.en.m.wikipedia.org/wiki/Ipswich

2006 Ipswich Murders.
- www.crimeandinvestigation.co.uk/crime-files/steve- wright-suffolk-strangler/timeline

Hadleigh Town.
- www.en.m.wikipedia.org/wiki/Hadleigh,_Suffolk

Traffic Count Data.
- www.dft.gov.uk/traffic-counts/cp.php?la=Suffolk

Orwell Bridge.
- www.highwaysengland.co.uk/orwell-bridge/

Suffolk County Councils Road Casualty reports of 2012-2016.
- www.suffolkroadsafe.com/about-suffolk-roadsafe/data

Road Casualties Great Britain, annual report: 2013.
- www.gov.uk/governement/statistics/reported-road- casualties-great-britain-annual-report-2013

Road Casualties Great Britain, annual report: 2015.

- www.gov.uk/government/statistics/reported-road-casualties-great-britain-annual-report-2015

Suffolk Police and Crime Commissioner: Road Safety report 2016/17.

Suffolk Police and Crime Commissioner: Road Safety report 2017/18.

- www.suffolk-pcc.gov.uk

East Anglian Air Ambulance.

- www.eaaa.org.uk

Roads Information.

- www.suffolk.gov.uk/assests/Roads-and-transport/how-we-manage-highway-maintenance/SALC

Suffolk Police Custody.

- www.suffolk.police.uk FOI 003969-17.

References

[1] Wikipedia – Suffolk 1466sq miles of area.
- www.en.m.wikipedia.org/wiki/suffolk
  21.03.2019

[2] Police Oath of Office.
- www.thebridgelifeinthemix.info/british-law/constable-oath/
  15.02.2019

[3] London Terror attack July 7th 2005.
- www.wikipedia.org/wiki/7_July_2005_London_Bombings
  18.12.2018

[4] Suffolk Police Grading Policy.
- www.suffolk.police.uk/sites/suffolk/files/ccr_call_grading.pdf
  08.01.2019

[5,6,7,8 & 9] Vehicle Stats.

- www.wikipedia.org/wiki/
  17.02.2019

[10] East Anglian Daily Times.

- www.eadt.co.uk/news/police-car-clocked-at-138mph-in-50mph-limit-while-in-pursuit-of-suspect-on-a140-at-coddenham-1-4049403
  13.11.2018

Sworn In

Jeremy H Cohen

I am a retired UK Police Officer, having worked for Suffolk Constabulary in the United Kingdom for over 13 years.

My career saw me spend 4 years as a general patrol officer in the busy town of Ipswich, 1 year in the smaller town of Hadleigh, and then over 8 years within the Specialist Operations Department, on the Roads Policing Unit.

During my career I was fortunate enough to receive a Chief Constables Commendation - the highest award offered internally by a Constabulary, a medal of appreciation from the then Prime Minister David Cameron and the Diamond Jubilee medal from HRH Queen Elizabeth II.

One achievement from my career comes with no medal, but a ring! Being a Police Officer enabled me to find my wife, the mother of my 2 children, who at the time of meeting her, volunteered in the Constabulary as a Special Constable. A moment of my life I cherish and another I am forever grateful to Suffolk Constabulary for. She has been there during the difficult times and how she has put up with me, I have no idea! I love her to bits.

My time within the Police Force saw me attend a vast myriad of incidents, ranging from petty theft to murder and rape, and then compiling subsequent prosecution files for the defendants to appear at court.

I would also become known as a Constabulary 'asset,' and an ambassador for the British Road Network due to my experience and training within the Roads Policing field. I was a qualified Police Class 1 Advanced Driver – the highest standard achievable within the United Kingdom, and a Police Pursuit Bronze Commander, which led me to be engaged in over 200 vehicle pursuits.

I became a scene manage for fatal and life-altering collisions and attended over 3000 minor to serious injury collisions, over 100 life-altering collisions and over 200 fatalities on the UK road network, where I would help ensure correct evidence was gathered and procedures followed to enable an accurate report on the collision being compiled, all the time ensuring other members of the public were inconvenienced the minimum amount of time necessary.

As a qualified vehicle examiner, I had to mechanically examine vehicles following a serious collision to ascertain if a defect had caused or contributed to a collision, and then present my evidence as fact to the British courts.

Leading on from fatal collisions I was trained as a Police Family Liaison Officer and would be assigned to a family following a fatal collision. My aim was to help families understand the collision, identify their deceased loved ones, explain the case paperwork to them and to assist them in understanding the process of an inquest into a person's death.

In my private life, I became an authorised instructor for the civilian-based 'Institute of Advanced Motorists' and also trained as a learner driver instructor.

This experience and training has given me a passion for road safety and also for mental health awareness amongst emergency service personnel. My goal is to pass this experience onto you by way of seeing what I had to go through and ultimately to effect a change, even a small change in people's minds when driving, and also when interacting with Law Enforcement Officers.

I am not done yet! My quest will continue...

Sworn In

Printed in Great Britain
by Amazon